D0574570

Exmoor

Compiled by
Sue Viccars

JARROLD
publishing

Mapping
sourced from Ordnance
Survey

Acknowledgements
For Emma, who really helped.

With grateful thanks to Brian Pearce
of Parracombe for so generously
sharing his in-depth knowledge of
Exmoor with me.

Text: Sue Viccars
Photography: Sue Viccars
Editorial: Ark Creative (UK) Ltd
Design: Ark Creative (UK) Ltd

© Jarrold Publishing, an imprint of
Pitkin Publishing Ltd

Jarrold Publishing
ISBN: 978-0-7117-4989-4

While every care has been taken to
ensure the accuracy of the route
directions, the publishers cannot
accept responsibility for errors or
omissions, or for changes in details
given. The countryside is not static:
hedges and fences can be removed,
field boundaries can alter, footpaths
can be rerouted and changes in
ownership can result in the closure or
diversion of some concessionary
paths. Also, paths that are easy and
pleasant for walking in fine conditions
may become slippery, muddy and
difficult in wet weather, while stepping
stones across rivers and streams may
become impassable.

If you find an inaccuracy in either the
text or maps, please write to or e-mail
Jarrold Publishing at one of the
addresses below.

First published 2003
by Jarrold Publishing
Revised and reprinted 2008

Printed in Singapore. 3/08

Pitkin Publishing Ltd
Healey House, Dene Road, Andover,
Hampshire SP10 2AA
e-mail: info@totalwalking.co.uk
www.totalwalking.co.uk

Front cover: Alamy (Jim Ritchie)
Previous page: Selworthy

Contents

Keymap

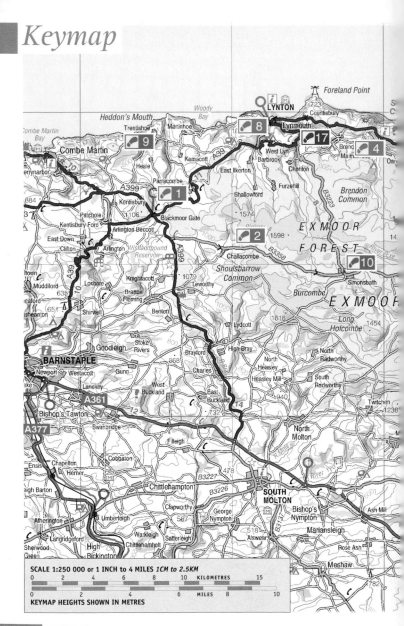

SCALE 1:250 000 or 1 INCH to 4 MILES *1CM to 2.5KM*

KEYMAP HEIGHTS SHOWN IN METRES

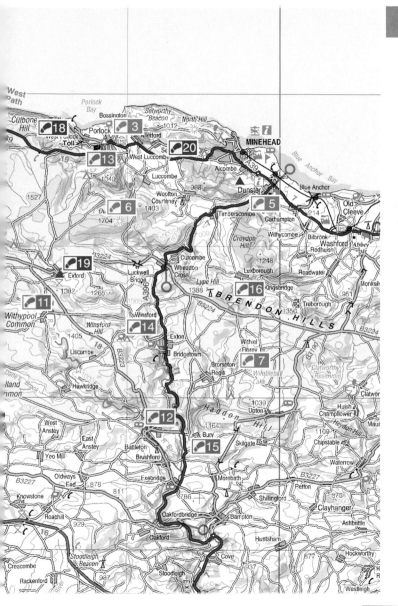

Introduction

So what sort of images does the word Exmoor bring to mind? Most people have heard of the Exmoor pony, or of R.D. Blackmore's *Lorna Doone*, or possibly of the long-distance walking and cycling route known as the Tarka Trail. But how many are aware of the fact that of all the British native breeds the Exmoor pony is the closest we have to the indigenous equine species? Or that you can actually visit the church where Lorna Doone was shot on her wedding day? Or that the Tarka Trail is named for the hero of North Devon author Henry Williamson's classic book *Tarka the Otter*, and is signed, most appropriately, with an otter paw? The fact is that Exmoor, with its fantastically varied landscapes, rich history, strong literary connections and fascinating wildlife, is an area that deserves intensive exploration. Less accessible and so less visited than many other outstandingly beautiful landscape areas in the south of England, those who do investigate Exmoor will find that its particular qualities draw them back time and time again.

A varied landscape

Exmoor, a moorland plateau straddling the north Devon/Somerset border and rising to 1,702ft (519m) at Dunkery Beacon, has a very different feel from the south-west's two other great uplands, Dartmoor in Devon and Bodmin Moor in Cornwall. These latter two are raised granite plateaux, capped by rugged, blocky tors, part of the same belt of ancient rock that finally outcrops to form the Isles of Scilly. Exmoor's underlying sedimentary Devonian sandstone, on the other hand, has produced moorlands that seem less remote and harsh than those of the granite uplands. The Exmoor landscape, including the ancient Forest of Exmoor to the west and the Brendon Hills to the east of the area, is altogether softer, smoother and rounder, with sweeping areas of heather moorland, deep, wooded combes (valleys) and a patchwork of small hedged fields, ancient farms and sheltered villages. Exmoor also has a real advantage over its moorland neighbours in that it has a superb northern boundary: a glorious stretch of unspoiled coastline, with soaring hog's-backed cliffs rising to almost 1,000ft (305m) in places and superb views over the Bristol Channel. But Exmoor is not without its

Exmoor National Park authority signpost on the Tarka Trail

harsher side. The early 18th-century writer Daniel Defoe described the moor as a 'filthie barren waste', in keeping with contemporary views of wilderness areas. Few would agree with that notion today, but parts of the landscape are certainly surprisingly dramatic. The notoriously boggy moorland around The Chains, lying 1,500ft (457.5m) above sea level and soaking up an annual rainfall of 80in (2,032mm), is definitely to be avoided when the mist is down. A prolonged spell of exceptionally heavy rainfall here in August 1952 produced the floodwaters that devastated the town of Lynmouth.

The human imprint

It would be easy to think that Exmoor is a totally natural landscape, but the moor has been settled since prehistoric times; there is evidence of Bronze Age occupation in the form of barrows and stone rows, and traces of Iron Age enclosures and hill forts. The origin of most of Exmoor's villages lie in the Saxon period, when the inhabitants were reliant on farming, and the wealth of early, remote churches at places such as Trentishoe and Stoke Pero indicate a time when the population was even more agriculturally based than today.

Interestingly two families have, in more recent times, been hugely influential in the shaping of the Exmoor landscape. From the 15th century onwards the benevolent Acland family owned several large estates and were much involved in improving conditions for the benefit of the local population, and in the early-19th century John Knight and his son Frederic attempted all kinds of abortive agricultural and industrial schemes. Although many of these failed, the Knights were reponsible for many of the typical features of the landscape today: farms, hedgebanks, walls, and beech woodlands.

Small-scale industrial development, too, has played its part in shaping the Exmoor landscape, most obviously in the Brendon Hills where iron was mined from Roman times until the end of the 19th century. The West Somerset Mineral Railway was built in 1856 to transport ore to the coast at Watchet.

Exmoor today

The great landscape and amenity value of Exmoor was recognised in the early 1950s when the Exmoor National Park was established to help conserve the area's natural beauty and wildlife, and is managed by the Exmoor National Park Authority from their headquarters at Exmoor House in Dulverton. The authority has the task of balancing the conflicting demands made on Exmoor: those of agriculture, tourism and conservation, and the increasingly controversial use of the moor for stag hunting in particular. All walkers should be aware of the reasons behind the setting up of National Parks in England and Wales (and shortly in Scotland too): the conservation of the natural beauty, wildlife and cultural heritage of the area, and the promotion of the understanding and enjoyment of its special qualities by the public.

Without doubt, the best way to explore and get a real understanding of Exmoor is on foot. The walks in this book have been devised to introduce the walker to a wide range of experiences, ranging from a gentle stroll through the deer park and woodland adjacent to the historic little town of Dunster, or through Lynton's extraordinary Valley of Rocks, to longer, more taxing routes on the edge of open moorland, beside sparkling rivers and along the switchback coast path. The routes suggested avoid the honeypot areas and concentrate instead on getting as far off the beaten track as quickly as possible, without necessitating the use of competent

Bury: medieval bridge over the River Haddeo

navigational skills. But it should be remembered that on any area of moorland weather can change rapidly, and fog and adverse conditions can occur all year round; *for this reason Walks 2, 6, 10, 11, 14 and 19 should not be attempted in inclement weather.*

With the introduction of **'gps enabled' walks,** you will see that this book now includes a list of waypoints alongside the description of the walk. We have included these so that you can enjoy the full benefits of gps should you wish to. Gps is an amazingly useful and entertaining navigational aid, and you do not need to be computer literate to enjoy it.

GPS waypoint co-ordinates add value to your walk. You will now have the extra advantage of introducing 'direction' into your walking which will enhance your leisure walking and make it safer. Use of a gps brings greater confidence and security and you will find you cover ground a lot faster should you need to.

For more detailed information on using your gps, a *Pathfinder Guide* introducing you to gps and digital mapping is now available. *GPS for Walkers*, written by experienced gps teacher and navigation trainer Clive Thomas, is available in bookshops (ISBN 978-0-7117-4445-5) or order online at www.totalwalking.co.uk

1 *Parracombe*

START Parracombe village
DISTANCE 2½ miles (4km)
TIME 1½ hours
PARKING Marked parking area by playing fields on right at top of village (when approaching from village centre; on left if approaching from north downhill from A39)
ROUTE FEATURES Some paths on farmland section of walk can be muddy

Parracombe is a very special place. Not only does it boast two churches and the remains of an old motte-and-bailey castle, it sits tucked away down narrow lanes as if miles from anywhere, yet lies within a stone's throw of the A39 from Blackmoor Gate to Lynmouth. This short exploration of the village and its surrounds would be a good leg-stretcher on a bright spring morning – before lunch at the pub.

There's a good deal of evidence of a long history of habitation in this area. A henge on **Parracombe Common,** near Woolhanger, dates from 2000BC, and there are Bronze Age remains: Chapman Barrows, Holwell Barrow, and the Longstone (in Challacombe parish). When the climate deteriorated towards the end of the Bronze Age the population moved into the valleys from the hills. Holwell Castle, the motte-and-bailey construction clearly visible during the latter part of the walk, dates from Norman times.

Turn right uphill out of the car park; 150 yds (137m) on turn right along a tree-lined track through an iron gate. The track passes the entrance to Heddon House, then becomes a woodland path, crosses a stream, and runs uphill to reach a tarmac lane on a corner.

A Turn left to cross the disused Lynton–Barnstaple narrow gauge railway line, opened in 1898 and closed in 1935. Turn left through the gate into the churchyard of St Petrock's Church. This is Churchtown, renowned for its perfectly preserved and wonderfully atmospheric old church of St Petrock: you just have to spend some time here. Leave the

PUBLIC TRANSPORT Bus services from Barnstaple, Lynton and Minehead
REFRESHMENTS Fox & Goose in Parracombe
PUBLIC TOILETS In car park
ORDNANCE SURVEY MAPS Explorer OL9 (Exmoor)

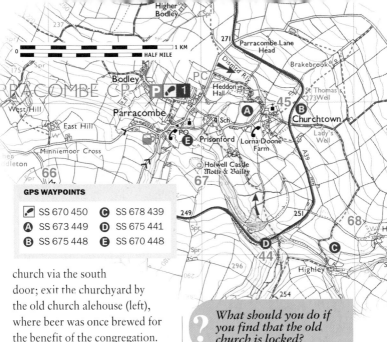

GPS WAYPOINTS

🖉 SS 670 450	**C** SS 678 439
A SS 673 449	**D** SS 675 441
B SS 675 448	**E** SS 670 448

church via the south
door; exit the churchyard by
the old church alehouse (left),
where beer was once brewed for
the benefit of the congregation.
Follow the track left uphill to meet
the A39.

B Cross the road (*take care*);
follow the bridleway signed
Parracombe Common past Lady's
Well (spring) on the right. The
bridleway forks left; keep right,
signed Highley. The grassy track
leads to a gate; pass through, then
downhill on a green lane (boggy in
winter). Pass through a gate into a
field; continue downhill. Pass
through the gate in the next fence.
Cross the gritty track; go through
two gates (wet). The path follows
the hedge on the right, zigzagging
downhill to lead into a green lane.

> **?** *What should you do if
> you find that the old
> church is locked?*

This meets the lane to Highley
Farm (left) via two gates.

C Turn left, following the
footpath sign. The lane crosses the
stream; turn right just before the
farmyard entrance, following
footpath signs through a gate/ford.
The path leads uphill with a
hedgebank right. At the top of the
hill turn right through a gate
(footpath sign). Keep the hedge on
the left; pass through an open
gateway at the end of the field, and
turn left. The hedgebank curves
away left; walk downhill across the
field to reach the lane via a stile.

Turn sharp right; follow the lane downhill, then uphill to meet the lane to Highley; turn left to the A39.

D Cross the road. Go through the gate, following the footpath sign ahead and over the dismantled railway line. Cross the next field, aiming for a yellow-topped post in the far right corner, then through a gate and over a stream into a rocky green lane. A few yards later turn left through a gate. Turn right, aiming for a gap in the fence, crossing a stream. Walk down the next field, passing a faded yellow blob on a tree on a wall corner right. Follow the hedgebank on the right; where it

bends away 90 degrees, turn right through the gate (footpath to Parracombe). Follow this green lane through a gate into the yard at Sunnyside. Follow the track ahead, turn left through a gate just past a big corrugated iron building (left). Cross the field, aiming for the church. Pass through a gate at the bottom of the field; keep right to cross the stream. Bear left uphill and over a stile onto the lane.

E Turn left; follow the lane to Christ Church and turn right to pass through the churchyard. Leave via the exit on the far side of the church, turn right and walk uphill to your car. ●

St Petrock's Church, Churchtown

Pinkworthy Pond

This is an easy walk that just has to be done on a bright, breezy summer's day when the skylarks are at their most vocal. There's a river to follow, a mysterious pond, superb views in every direction, and a terrific feeling of space up on The Chains. But do not attempt this one in mist, or after heavy rainfall.

2

START Goat Hill Bridge on the B3358
DISTANCE 3 miles (4.8km)
TIME 1½ hours
PARKING Unsurfaced parking area on the right of the road just east of bridge (NB There are two parking areas: use the second one when travelling towards Challacombe)
ROUTE FEATURES Can be boggy in places

Pinkworthy, or Pinkery, Pond lies in an area of Exmoor known as The Chains, a notoriously peaty and boggy place that acts like a giant sponge, soaking up much of the high moor's annual rainfall of 80in (2,032mm). The rivers Exe, Barle and West Lyn, among others, rise here. In August 1952, 9in (228mm) of rainfall in a 24-hour period on The Chains produced the floodwaters that devastated the coastal town of Lynmouth *(see Walk 17)*.

From the parking area walk along the grass verge west towards Goat Hill Bridge. Turn right through the small wooden gate at the bridge, and up the tarmac way towards Pinkery Outdoor Education Centre: note the tiny River Barle to your left.

A When the lane rises steeply towards the centre, turn left, signed 'Pinkery Pond and The Chains'. Follow the path through a gateway to the left of a copse. Keep straight ahead along the contours of the hill, passing to the left of the wind generator, and aiming for a small gate in the hedgebank ahead. The path then becomes more obvious and runs across open moorland; parts are boggy and there are boardwalks. At a fork bear right

PUBLIC TRANSPORT None available
REFRESHMENTS Black Venus Inn, Challacombe, 1½ miles (2.4km) west on the B3358
PUBLIC TOILETS None on route
ORDNANCE SURVEY MAPS Explorer OL9 (Exmoor)

uphill; look ahead to see the turf and stone dam across the valley.

The path runs up the right side of the dam, through which the Barle gushes via a waterfall. Pass through the wooden gate **B** in the fence to have a closer look at the pond, one of John Knight's 'white elephants'.

GPS WAYPOINTS

🖉 SS 724 403		**C**	SS 731 418
A SS 723 410		**D**	SS 734 419
B SS 723 422		**E**	SS 729 401

It was dug out by hand by 200 Irish navvies around 1830, but no one is quite sure why. It's said that around 100 years ago a local farmer out riding his horse disappeared; the pond was drained (there was a huge plughole at the base of the dam) and his body was found at the bottom. Look out for the rocky tunnel to the right of the path leading to the water's edge: it's possible to scramble through to the other side of the dam (if you're wearing wellingtons).

Retrace your steps back through the gate and turn left to walk along The Chains. At the next gate

In 1818 John Knight, a Worcestershire entrepreneur, bought about 10,000 acres (4,050 hectares) of the **Royal Forest of Exmoor** from the Crown. He later extended his estate even further. He planned to improve the agricultural potential of the land, but most of his schemes were unsuccessful. His son Frederic continued his efforts and also attempted to exploit local sources of copper and iron. The Knights were responsible for many of the features so characteristic of this part of Exmoor today: farms, lanes, hedgebanks, walls and beech woodlands.

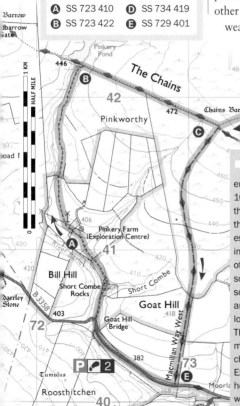

Pinkworthy – pronounced 'Pinkery' – Pond

in the bank, turn left through the gate and immediately right, and right again through a second wooden gate, then left to follow the bank again. Stay on the right of the bank/wire fence – it is a little less boggy on this side.

C At the next gate on the left an Exmoor National Park Authority signpost reveals that you are on the Tarka Trail, which runs for 180 miles (290km) from Okehampton, on the edge of Dartmoor, to the north coast at Ilfracombe and Lynton. *Turn left here and cross open moorland if you want to visit Bronze Age Chains Barrow* **D**

> **?** Which animal paw print can be seen on a wooden post during part **C** of the walk, and what does it signify?

(1,598ft/487m above sea level), from which there are magnificent views in every direction. If not, turn right and follow the signed bridleway downhill, passing the occasional blue-topped post and aiming for a line of trees at the bottom of the meadow. About two-thirds down the field you cross a small earthwork, all that remains of John Knight's proposed (but never completed) 'canal'. Just past the last post, look ahead to a gate in the field corner with a blue-topped post. Go through and continue left to follow the wall and beech trees downhill. Pass through a five-bar gate into the next field, and keep straight on downhill to meet the road via a small gate **E**. Turn right to walk through the first parking area, then onto the second and your car. ●

3 *Bossington*

START Bossington

DISTANCE 2¼ miles (3.6km)

TIME 1¼ hours

PARKING Car park (contributions cairn) in Bossington

ROUTE FEATURES Steep path downhill through woods to North Bridge

A simple little walk from the picturesque National Trust village of Bossington out to the rugged headland of Hurlstone Point, with fantastic views over Porlock Bay. It is perhaps most lovely on a warm summer's evening when the shadows lengthen over the broad Vale of Porlock. The route crosses the South West Coast Path, which has been diverted inland and rejoins the coast at Porlock Weir.

From the car park pass the information board and walk over the double-railed wooden footbridge (North Bridge) over the Horner Water (which rises 8 miles/12.9km inland and filters through the shingle ridge to the sea), following signs for Hurlstone. Turn left following bridlepath and coast path signs along a broad, earthy woodland track, with the stream on the left, passing an idyllic green-painted timber house complete with veranda on the right. Views of Bossington beach – and frequently of sea fishermen – open up left;

In Saxon times **Bossington** belonged to the abbey of Athelney. Today it lies within the Holnicote Estate, which was given by the Acland family to the National Trust in 1944 *(see Walk 20)*. Bossington village is extremely picturesque, with creamy-yellow limewashed 14th- and 15th-century cottages lining the quiet, narrow lanes. Many are built in traditional local style, with tall chimney stacks and round bread ovens.

the remains of limekilns can be seen behind the beach, set up by the Aclands in the 18th century. Coal and limestone were shipped in from south Wales and burnt to

PUBLIC TRANSPORT Bus service from Minehead

REFRESHMENTS Picnic area by car park; seasonal tearooms in Bossington; range of pubs and cafés in Porlock

PUBLIC TOILETS In car park

ORDNANCE SURVEY MAPS Explorer OL9 (Exmoor)

'Roses over the door' in Bossington village

the beach 65–100ft (20–30m) inland and creating a saltwater marsh, it has been decided to let Nature take its course. Pass the NT cairn and leave the South West Coast Path (which runs for 630 miles/1,014km from Minehead in Somerset to Poole in Dorset) where it ascends steeply right up Hurlstone Combe. Walk ahead and follow the rising path to reach Hurlstone Point and the old

produce lime for limewash, and for fertiliser to improve the acidic Exmoor soils for agricultural purposes.

A Leave the wooded path via a five-bar gate and onto the lower slopes of Bossington Hill; note Western gorse and bell heather. Look left for superb views along the shingle bank of Porlock Ridge (SSSI) towards Porlock Weir *(see Walk 18)* and Worthy Wood beyond. Over the past 8,000 years occasional westerly and north-westerly gales have shifted pebbles eastwards to create first a spit, then a bar, enclosing the land behind. When storms breached the bank it would be rebuilt to protect the pastures and freshwater marshes behind it. Since a huge storm in October 1996 breached the bank, pushing

GPS WAYPOINTS

SS 897 480   **B** SS 899 491

A SS 897 487   **C** SS 900 481

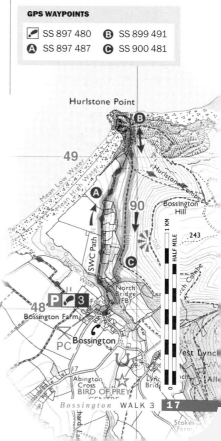

coastguard lookout **B**, strengthened during the Second World War to withstand gunnery practice. Retrace your steps; where the path forks, take the left path and walk on to cross the coast path a little above the NT cairn and noticeboard. Walk straight on, signed 'Allerford', enjoying beautiful views over Bossington and Porlock, and inland towards Horner Wood (*see Walk 13*) and Horner Hill. This lovely, level path runs through gorse and bracken along the contour.

? *What sort of fish can be found in Horner Water?*

C At the edge of a sycamore wood turn sharp right signed 'Bossington'; follow the rocky path steeply downhill. Pass through a gate, then zigzag downhill to North Bridge, where there is also a ford. Turn left over the bridge and back to the car park. ●

Looking towards Bossington and Hurlstone Point from Porlock Hill

Malmsmead and Oare

START Malmsmead
DISTANCE 2½ miles (4km)
TIME 1½ hours
PARKING Car park (charge) in Malmsmead
ROUTE FEATURES No difficulties

4

Visit Malmsmead on a sunny summer's day and you would be forgiven for thinking that the whole place is nothing more than a creation for the tourist industry. But apart from various links with R.D. Blackmore's story of Lorna Doone, *there is much natural beauty to be enjoyed on this gentle walk through the tranquil valleys of the Badgworthy and Oare Waters.*

R.D. Blackmore based his novel **Lorna Doone**, published in 1869 but set in the days of the Monmouth Rebellion, on the local tradition of a band of infamous outlaws – the Doones – living perhaps in Hoccombe Combe, a tributary of Badgworthy Water. Blackmore used local names and places in his novel, so much so that today it is quite hard to distinguish fact from fiction. His heroine Lorna was kidnapped by the Doones.

Leave the car park; turn left and at the first lane junction keep ahead on the lane signed Fullingscott etc. Walk uphill; where the lane bears right keep ahead through a gate **A** onto the bridleway to Badgworthy Valley. The track undulates along the valley side before dropping towards Cloud Farm and passing through a gate. Turn left **B** on the footpath to Oare Church, crossing Badgworthy Water (the boundary between Devon and Somerset) via a footbridge. Walk uphill through the campsite and cross the drive

? *What are R.D. Blackmore's birth and death dates?*

PUBLIC TRANSPORT None available
REFRESHMENTS Café (seasonal) at Malmsmead and at Cloud Farm; picnic area by car park and at Oare village hall
PUBLIC TOILETS In car park
ORDNANCE SURVEY MAPS Explorer OL9 (Exmoor)

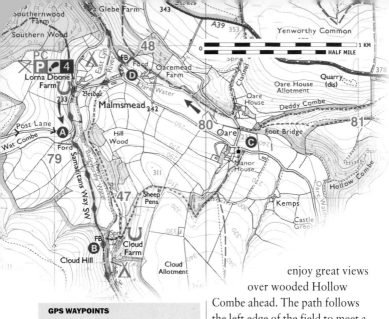

GPS WAYPOINTS

✏ SS 791 477	**C** SS 804 472
A SS 791 474	**D** SS 794 477
B SS 793 467	

(farm and tearoom right). Turn left onto a track just before the telephone box. Pass through a gate into a stableyard; follow yellow footpath arrows left under a big barn, through a gate and up a grassy track. Pass through a five-bar gate: look back for superb views down the valley towards Badgworthy Hill, beneath which the remains of a medieval village can be found. The track bears right away from the valley. There's a wonderfully airy feel up here; pass through a gate, and enjoy great views over wooded Hollow Combe ahead. The path follows the left edge of the field to meet a stock fence; pass through a five-bar gate round the edge of a small combe. Where the track bears away from the combe follow yellow markers ahead and downhill. Pass through a gate in the next wall and down the edge of the meadow. At the bottom of the field turn right following the footpath sign, then left through the gate. Continue down the field to meet the lane through a five-bar gate.

C Turn left to pass Oare Church. At the junction of lanes (Oare Manor left) turn right. Cross the 18th-century bridge; a little up the hill, just past the drive to 19th-century Oare House (right), turn left through a gate down a bridlepath, signed 'Malmsmead'. Pass through the field, aiming for a gate leading into a larch plantation. Leave the trees via a metal gate, and keep straight ahead, passing through a gate to the right of a bungalow. Pass through a gate by the yard; walk straight on, through another gate. Pass through a gate at the end of the next field and turn left (signed 'Malmsmead') to meet the Oare Water. Cross the river on a railed concrete bridge. Follow the path uphill through a five-bar gate to meet the lane.

D Turn right to walk past Oare village hall (1930), since 1977

Oare **Church of St Mary the Virgin** dates back 1,000 years. The interior is simple, with boxed wooden pews. A superb wooden buzzard supports the lectern, carved by a local craftsman, and replaces the previous one, a golden eagle, which was stolen. The church was the setting for the marriage of Jan Ridd to Lorna Doone in Blackmore's novel. The memorial to Richard Doddridge Blackmore, whose grandfather was rector at Oare from 1809–42, is a replica of the original in Exeter Cathedral.

home to the Exmoor Natural History Society Field Centre, open two/three days a week. Pass over the 17th-century packhorse bridge next to the ford over Badgworthy Water, which is joined by the Oare Water just to the north to form the East Lyn. To the right stands Lorna Doone Farm, part of which dates from Saxon times. In the novel the ancestors of Nicholas Snowe, a church warden at Oare, lived here; the building now houses a gift shop. Pass the Devon county sign, and return to your car. ●

View of Oare House from Oare Church

5 *Dunster*

The picturesque little medieval town of Dunster can get horribly crowded at holiday time. You can leave it all behind on this walk, which gives you a chance to explore the old deer park in peace, with fabulous views over the castle and town and, from Gallax Hill – site of Iron Age activity, and with the public gallows on its lower slopes in times past – inland towards Dunkery Beacon. This is a walk full of surprises.

START Dunster

DISTANCE 2¾ miles (4.4km)

TIME 1½ hours

PARKING Park Street car park off A396 (Pay and Display)

ROUTE FEATURES Steep trudge up Park Lane; steep (sometimes muddy) descent through woods from Gallax Hill

Dunster Castle was given to the National Trust by the Luttrell family in 1976, but there has been a castle here since Norman times; the oldest part of the castle dates from the 13th century. It has been considerably modified since. There was extensive rebuilding during the 19th century under the ownership of the Luttrells, who bought it in 1376. During the Civil War the castle was a Royalist stronghold, and withstood a siege that lasted 160 days.

From the car park turn left past pretty cottages to cross the River Avill (from the Saxon word for apple) via double-arched Gallox Bridge, a medieval packhorse bridge. At the junction of paths keep straight on to pass thatched cottages (right).

Ⓐ At the next junction of paths (at the entrance to the deer park, enclosed by Henry Fownes Luttrell in the mid 18th century), turn left through the kissing-gate. You now have a choice of three paths: take the one on the left, signed 'Carhampton'. The path rises up through wonderful undulating parkland, with lovely views right over the castle and watermill. Note the frequent 'bumps' in the ground,

PUBLIC TRANSPORT Bus service from Minehead and Tiverton

REFRESHMENTS Range of pubs and cafés in Dunster; tearoom/garden at Dunster Water Mill (seasonal)

PUBLIC TOILETS In Dunster

PLAY AREA Packhorse Playing Field by Gallox Bridge

ORDNANCE SURVEY MAPS Explorer OL9 (Exmoor)

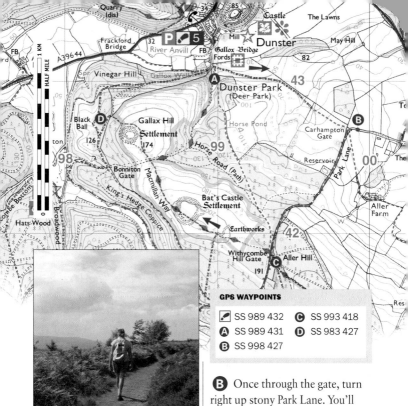

The map shows the area around Dunster, including Dunster Castle, Dunster Park (Deer Park), Gallax Hill Settlement, Bat's Castle Settlement, Withycombe Hill Gate, and Aller Hill, with GPS waypoints marked A–D.

GPS WAYPOINTS

🥾 SS 989 432	**C** SS 993 418
A SS 989 431	**D** SS 983 427
B SS 998 427	

The lovely path to Bat's Castle in late summer

which are grassed over anthills: this area has been uncultivated for hundreds of years. Follow the path over the crest of the hill and through a wooden gate by a single oak tree. Continue up the next hill to reach Carhampton Gate.

B Once through the gate, turn right up stony Park Lane. You'll probably hear the whistle of the restored steam engine of the West Somerset Railway; it runs from Bishops Lydeard to Minehead, between Dunster and the coast. Park Lane climbs steeply through dark woodland to reach Withycombe Hill Gate, where there is a junction of paths.

C Turn right through the gate; keep ahead, signed 'permitted path to Bat's Castle'. Walk straight on through a larch plantation out into

Dunster Watermill, dating from medieval times, has been a grist mill since the 18th century, and has also been a cloth mill. It can be found by turning right from the car park, and then right again opposite the mill leat. Dunster had a profitable woollen industry until the 18th century (as also evidenced by the old Yarn Market in the main street). This working mill, owned by the National Trust, has been sympathetically restored, and has a very pretty tea garden.

? *How high above sea level do you think you are when you reach Bat's Castle hill fort?*

the open, to reach earthworks via a staggered wooden barrier. Follow the path along the top of the hill to cross the circular ditch and rampart enclosing Bat's Castle Iron Age hill fort, set on a fantastic vantage-point. Dating from 400–100BC, the site has not been excavated, but

comprises 3½ acres (1.4 ha) within a double rampart. It is thought the inhabitants occupied circular thatched huts, kept cattle and sheep, and cultivated barley and spelt (wheat). Continue over the next ditch/rampart and follow the path downhill through light woodland and bracken to join an offshoot of the Macmillan Way (Boston, Lincolnshire, to Abbotsbury, Dorset). This 'extension' runs for 102 miles (164km) from Castle Cary in Somerset to Barnstaple in Devon. Follow the path uphill to pass another earthwork (left), after which the path drops to enter thicker woodland.

D At the muddy junction of paths, turn right *before* the gate and stile. The path runs downhill, with a wall along the edge of the trees left, then passes into laurel and rhododendron to meet a woodland track. Turn right on the bridlepath down Vinegar Hill to reach **A**. Turn right to find the River Avill at Gallox Bridge; cross over, walk up the lane and back to your car. ●

Looking along the High Street towards the castle, Dunster

Dunkery Beacon

START Car park at Lang Combe Head (free)

DISTANCE 3 miles (4.8km)

TIME 1½ hours

PARKING Unmarked car park at Lang Combe Head, Stoke Pero Common

ROUTE FEATURES Steep climb up lane to return to your car

This is definitely one for a hot summer's day, when the buzzing of bees and the heady scent of heather and gorse fill the soft air. It's a really lovely walk to Exmoor's highest point – the views are fabulous – with a good smattering of archaeological interest, too. Do the walk in August, when the moors are covered in a rich carpet of purple and yellow flowers.

The **whortleberry** (Somerset's name for the wild bilberry) grows in abundance here. Known as the whimberry in Wales, and the blaeberry in Scotland, in the early 20th century collecting these berries for sale was an important source of additional income for local families; schools would give children time off to help. The berries were packed in punnets for transport to London and the Midlands to be used in the food industry (being rich in vitamins C and D), or as a dye for RAF uniforms.

Follow the track to pass the Bronze Age cairn (burial mound) of Great Rowbarrow on the left **Ⓐ**; the

From Dunkery Beacon towards Porlock Bay

From the car park follow the gritty track running away from the road. This walk has a wonderfully airy and open feel – you're really on top of the world.

PUBLIC TRANSPORT None available

REFRESHMENTS None on route

PUBLIC TOILETS None on route

ORDNANCE SURVEY MAPS Explorer OL9 (Exmoor)

The rolling moorland of this part of Exmoor is a sight for sore eyes in late summer. Purple ling (common heather), crimson-purple **bell heather** and the slightly lighter **cross-leaved heath**, along with bright yellow tormentil, and gold **Western gorse**, can be found here. At one time there were black grouse on these moors, but the last sighting was in 1981; a few **red grouse** remain.

track then bears left along the top of the hill past Little Rowbarrow. During this period (from *c.*1500BC) increasing areas of woodland were cleared for pasture and crops, implying a more settled population, as evidenced by traces of farmsteads and enclosures on the high moorland. Keep slightly uphill towards the beacon, crossing a bridlepath en route.

B Dunkery Beacon lies 1,702ft (519m) above sea level, and can be seen for many miles around. Consequently the views from the summit are stunning: it is said that on a clear day you can see as far as the Malvern Hills in Worcestershire. The coast of south Wales to the north seems incredibly close, and the islands of Flat Holm and Steep Holm in the mouth of the Severn beyond Bridgwater Bay are visible to the north-east. The name 'Dunkery' comes from the old English *dun* – hill, and the

GPS WAYPOINTS

📷 SS 870 419	**C** SS 886 415
A SS 875 415	**D** SS 878 424
B SS 891 415	

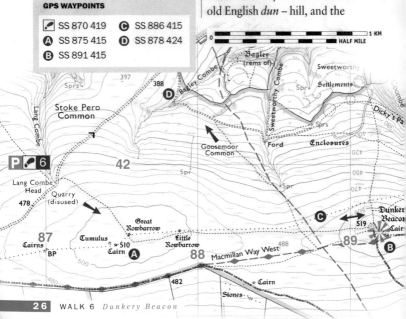

The view east from Goosemoor Common

Common, with lovely views over the Horner Valley towards Porlock. You may be lucky enough to see red deer on the moorland slopes above Aller Combe. The path reaches Dicky's Path (a track – many of the paths within the Holnicote Estate were named after members of the Acland family) at an angle. Turn left and follow the track through a group of small hawthorns, dropping to cross a stream at Bagley Combe. Stop here. The track runs on uphill and right to pass traces of a settlement at Bagley that dates from Domesday until the late 19th century. At Sweetworthy, a little to the east, can be found the remains of an Iron Age hillslope enclosure, a small agricultural settlement.

Celtic *creag* – rocky place. A cairn just by the beacon commemorates the donation of Dunkery Hill to the National Trust (much of it was originally part of the Holnicote Estate), and a viewpoint indicator provides added interest. Beacons such as this were originally set up across England to provide an early warning system at the time of the Spanish Armada in the summer of 1588. To leave, retrace your steps to where the bridlepath crosses the outward route. (*Note: If you want to avoid a steep trudge up the lane at the end of the walk, go straight on here and retrace your steps to your car.*)

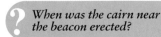

? **When was the cairn near the beacon erected?**

C Turn right downhill and follow the path across Goosemoor

D Immediately over the stream turn left on a narrow grassy path. Where this path appears to bend left to run into the head of the hollow, keep right uphill under hawthorn trees. The path becomes indistinct, but continue uphill to meet the lane. Turn left and climb steeply back to your car. ●

7 *Withiel Florey*

START Wimbleball Lake (north end)

DISTANCE 3 miles (4.8km)

TIME 1½ hours

PARKING Car park (free) near Bessom Bridge

ROUTE FEATURES Steep slightly overgrown path downhill through Edgerton Plantation; unmarked footpath through Cophole Farm land

A very gentle walk – and one where you're very unlikely to see anyone else – along the edge of the peaceful northern waters of Wimbleball Lake to the remote little church at Withiel Florey. If you want to avoid an easy but slightly lengthy walk along the lane back to your car – and a tricky stream crossing and boggy ground – retrace your steps from the church and return via the outward route.

[👟] Turn left onto the road; turn left at Bessom Cross and walk over Bessom Bridge, with lovely views over Wimbleball Lake and Haddon Hill to the left.

Ⓐ Once over the bridge, turn right into Hurscombe Nature Reserve. Go through a gate, up steps, turn right and follow the track high above the most northerly arm of Wimbleball Lake. The reserve covers 49 acres (19.8 hectares) of scrub, marsh, rough grassland, old woodland and water, and deciduous trees planted since 1976. The path drops down and

The scattered agricultural hamlet of **Withiel Florey** lies within the parish of Brompton Regis, formerly known as King's Brompton. The Church of the Blessed Virgin Mary dates from the 13th century, but was heavily restored in 1853. In the wall opposite the church gates is an old well, no longer working, dated 29 September 1817. In medieval times Brompton Regis was a prosperous market town, as evidenced by the division of the village into Higher and Lower Town.

curves away from the water, passes through a gate and over a stream to leave the reserve. Follow the track along the edge of the field and

PUBLIC TRANSPORT None available

REFRESHMENTS None on route; café (seasonal) at Cowlings at Wimbleball Lake; the George Inn at Brompton Regis

PUBLIC TOILETS None on route; at Cowlings at Wimbleball Lake

ORDNANCE SURVEY MAPS Explorer OL9 (Exmoor)

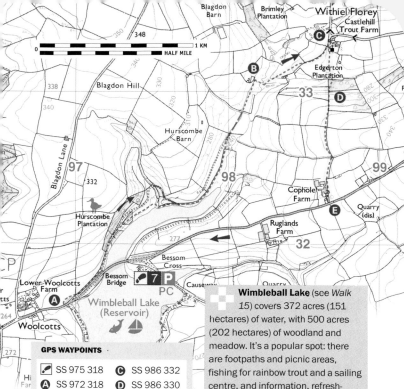

GPS WAYPOINTS

📷 SS 975 318 **C** SS 986 332
A SS 972 318 **D** SS 986 330
B SS 981 330 **E** SS 986 322

Wimbleball Lake (see *Walk 15*) covers 372 acres (151 hectares) of water, with 500 acres (202 hectares) of woodland and meadow. It's a popular spot: there are footpaths and picnic areas, fishing for rainbow trout and a sailing centre, and information, refreshments and camping at Cowlings on the western shore. The area attracts a wide variety of wildlife, and overwintering birds include wigeon, teal, pochard and tufted duck.

through a gate at the hilltop; keep straight on through another gate to re-enter the reserve at the water's edge. Follow the path north to leave the open water, and through a line of ash trees. At the end of the field go over a stile/gate; straight on and over another stile in a wire fence. Look ahead right to a post with a blue splodge; once past that, walk towards the bottom right corner of the field, bear left round gorse bushes and through a gate

over a stream in the hedgebank. Walk straight through the next field, with the stream and later a ford right.

B When level with a banked/beech-lined enclosure on the left (actually the ruins of Hurscombe Farm – though looking far more sinister than that), turn

Wimbleball Lake as seen from above Bessom Bridge

but look out for the occasional yellow splodge. Walk straight across the field to meet a stile in the fence, 20 yds (18m) left of a solitary hawthorn tree marking the edge of Edgerton Plantation. Pick your way carefully and steeply

right to cross the river on a wooden railed footbridge. About 10 yds (9m) beyond the bridge bear left, aiming for a post on top of a small hillock, crossing a small stream en route. Just before the post the limewashed tower of Withiel Florey church comes into view ahead. Continue to the top corner of the field; turn right through the gate, then left and walk along the hedge to a five-bar gate opposite Castlehill Trout Farm. Turn right for the remote and simple little 14th-century Church of St Mary Magdalene.

> **?** **What isn't allowed to cross the footbridge at the start of point B?**

C From the south door leave the churchyard via a stile in the hedge. *Note: there are no footpath signs*

downhill to cross the stream via a fallen tree, then cross boggy ground straight ahead to meet a track **D**. Walk straight on uphill, keeping the line of beech trees immediately right. Cross another track; keep straight on through a gate into a field, and immediately right through a gate. Turn left and walk along the top edge of the field. Walk through the next gate, with great views of Wimbleball to the right. At the end of that field, pass through a gate; at the end of that field go through a gate in the corner, then immediately left through another. Take the first gate right opposite the farmyard; turn left down the drive of Cophole Farm.

E Turn right and follow the road downhill to Bessom Cross; turn left then right to your car. ●

The Valley of Rocks

8

START	Valley of Rocks
DISTANCE	2¼ miles (3.6km)
TIME	1¼ hours
PARKING	Exmoor National Park car park in the Valley of Rocks (contributions cairn)
ROUTE FEATURES	No difficulties

An easy walk that explores the unexpectedly rugged landscape of the Valley of Rocks, and the once isolated but now bustling community of Lynton, with stunning views inland across the wooded valley of the East Lyn river and over the little town of Lynmouth and the sea towards lofty Countisbury Hill; and with the chance of a ride on the cliff railway thrown in!

Lynton, mentioned in *Domesday* and formerly a small community relying on sheep farming and spinning, and Lynmouth, a little fishing port, developed as tourist destinations from the end of the 18th century when the Romantic Movement brought such locations into fashion and the Napoleonic Wars restricted travel on the continent. The dramatic cliffs, wooded valleys and sparkling rivers attracted hordes of visitors; in the late 19th century many new houses and hotels were built, and the area became known as 'Little Switzerland'.

Walk uphill along the back of the car park; turn right through a break in the wall. Look back at the rocky ridge towards the coast; this strange valley is full of legend and superstition. The rock formation called Rugged Jack, ahead and left, is named after the leader of a group of revellers, said to have been turned to stone by the Devil; Chimney Rock, straight ahead, is where wreckers used to set lights to lure ships onto the rocks in the 18th century.

A Turn left through a kissing-gate; follow the footpath uphill. Look across the valley to the steep zigzag path up Hollerday Hill,

PUBLIC TRANSPORT Bus service (to Lynton) from Barnstaple, Ilfracombe, Minehead and Taunton
REFRESHMENTS Range of cafés and pubs in Lynton: Mother Meldrum's tea gardens and restaurant (seasonal) in the Valley of Rocks; picnic area in car park
PUBLIC TOILETS In car park, and in Lynton
ORDNANCE SURVEY MAPS Explorer OL9 (Exmoor)

800ft (244m) above sea level, and site of an Iron Age hill fort. The deeply banked path levels off to pass above the cemetery (left). Pass a footpath to Lee Abbey (right), and cross a stream to reach Lydiate Lane opposite Park Farm.

B Turn left downhill to meet the road on a sharp bend. Turn left downhill; turn left along Crossmead, then right on Lee Road to pass the Convent of the Poor Clares (1910). This order of contemplative nuns was founded by St Clare, a follower of St Francis of Assisi. Follow the road downhill to pass Lynton and Lynmouth Town Hall. Just beyond is the path to Hollerday Hill, the old drive to Hollerday House, where local benefactor George Newnes lived in the 19th century; the house burned down in mysterious circumstances in 1913. Continue through the town, passing the entrance to the Cliff Railway (left), and the Victorian edifice of the

> The **Valley of Rocks** is one of the most dramatic sites on Exmoor. The valley, which unusually runs parallel to the sea, is now dry; it is thought that it originally held one or both of the two Lyn rivers, but that coastal erosion altered the course to its current position, entering the sea at Lynmouth. Freeze–thaw action during the Ice Age is responsible for creating the weird and jagged sandstone tors that rise craggily above the valley, and for the large amounts of scree on the hillslopes.

GPS WAYPOINTS

🖊	SS 719 497	**C**	SS 720 494
A	SS 711 496	**D**	SS 705 497
B	SS 714 492		

Valley of Rocks Hotel (left).

C Turn left along North Walk Hill, leading to the North Promenade built in 1817, 10 years after the construction of Lynton's first hotel. St Mary's Church of the Virgin is opposite; the tower dates from the 13th century, but the building is late 19th century.

The amazing Cliff Railway

Continue down the North Walk – the Coast Path from Lynmouth joins right – and cross the Cliff Railway. This amazing 900ft (275m) long water-powered railway opened in 1890, the steepest railway in the world at that time; its gradient is 1 in 1¾. Continue along the tarmac path and through a gate onto the open cliffs, with a very steep drop to the sea right. Look out for Lynton's famous wild Cheviot goats, introduced in 1976 to replace the feral goats that have roamed this area for centuries. Pass a path to Hollerday Hill left; continue on for a great view of towering Castle Rock (said to be site of an ancient castle, whose inhabitants were driven out by the Devil), and the folly of Duty Point Tower beyond.

Follow the path inland; take the first rocky path left **D**, and follow it up the valley to pass through the fee-paying car park. Meet the road, turn left past the café (Mother Meldrum featured in R.D. Blackmore's *Lorna Doone* – *see Walk 4* – and is thought to be based on a witch, Aggie Norman, who lived in the valley in the early 19th century) and return to the car park. Note Modelgate Shelter opposite, displaying lovely panels of mosaic quotes from poems by Southey, Wordsworth, Shelley and Coleridge, who all visited the area in the 18th/19th centuries. ●

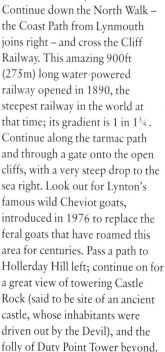

What is the weight limit for the bridge over the Cliff Railway, and what will happen to you if you exceed it?

9 *Trentishoe*

START Trentishoe Down
DISTANCE 3½ miles (5.6km)
TIME 2 hours
PARKING car park on Trentishoe Down (free)
ROUTE FEATURES Coast path narrow in places

Although only a third of Exmoor National Park lies within Devon, the county is blessed with more than half the National Park coastline, and this route explores one of the most dramatic sections: the cliffs west of Heddon's Mouth, rising over 650ft (200m), are some of the highest in the country. This inspiring walk takes in the tiny church at remote Trentishoe, then returns on a glorious, gentle path above the hanging oak woodlands of the Heddon Valley.

🥾 Walk away from the road downhill between two wooden benches on a broad, grassy path to meet the coast path, signed right for Heddon's Mouth.

Ⓐ Turn right, with brilliant views ahead across Heddon's Mouth Cleave towards the site of the Roman signal station (the Beacon) and the hamlet of Martinhoe on the coastal hill towering above Heddon's Mouth. At the next coast path sign fork right to leave the path, signed County Road, and walk uphill, later with a hedgebank left. Where the wall runs away left, keep straight on to reach the parking area at Holdstone Down

Cross. Holdstone Down, to the west, rises to 1,143ft (349m) and is one of the highest coastal hills in south-west England. Walk on to meet the road.

Ⓑ Turn first left down the narrow lane (*Note: The sign to Trentishoe church points back over the cliffs – ignore it.*). This quiet lane runs gently downhill, with lovely views over the deep wooded valleys inland. The National Trust owns 2000 acres (810ha) of land in this area, and there is a good information centre (and ice cream) near the Hunter's Inn. Much of the area, which comprises extensive oak woodland, deep valleys, coastal

PUBLIC TRANSPORT None available
REFRESHMENTS Hunter's Inn in Heddon Valley
PUBLIC TOILETS None on route; in Heddon Valley
ORDNANCE SURVEY MAPS Explorer OL9 (Exmoor)

Until the chancel was added towards the end of the 19th century, **Trentishoe** was said to be the smallest church in Devon *(see Walk 18)*. There is a record of a church here as early as 1260. The squat, castellated tower dates from the 15th century, and there is a lovely minstrels' gallery, built in 1771. Look out for the gravestone of an unusual 'resident' – David (Dick) Turpin, organist for 20 years – and his wife Violet, which lies near the south door.

heath and high cliffs, is a designated SSSI. The Heddon Valley holds a wide variety of wildlife, including the rare high brown fritillary butterfly. Follow the lane down to find the tiny hamlet of Trentishoe, with the Church of St Peter above the lane on the left **C**. This tranquil spot feels a million miles away from civilisation, but R.D. Blackmore featured Trentishoe in his novel *Clara Vaughan* in 1864, and 96 people were recorded living here in 1891. In early summer the graveyard is awash with bluebells, lady's smock and ramsons.

From the church continue down the lane to pass a couple of houses on the left. Turn left **D**, following an 'access to coast path' sign on Trentishoe Combe. This lovely path runs along the edge of the Heddon Valley; the deep cleft in the cliffs at Heddon's Mouth comes into view. The land to east and west of Heddon's Mouth rises to an incredible

GPS WAYPOINTS

✏ SS 627 479		**C**	SS 646 486
A SS 628 481		**D**	SS 647 484
B SS 635 479		**E**	SS 649 491

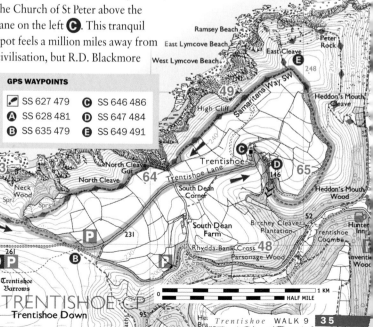

The coast path near Neck Wood, looking east towards Heddon's Mouth

820ft (250m), and the slopes are covered with scree, created by freeze – thaw action on the underlying sandstone. The cliffs to the east of Heddon's Mouth hold one of only two colonies of razorbill, guillemot and kittiwake in north Devon. There is a restored limekiln by the small beach at Heddon's Mouth; landing places are scarce on this rugged coast, and there are tales of smuggling here in the past. The path runs on to meet the coast path above East Cleave.

E Turn left along the coast path. Turn left through a gate where signed, then right along the edge of the field signed Combe Martin, then through a gate to regain the cliff edge. Keep on the coast path and go through a gate above Neck Wood. The path runs across a field; continue straight ahead uphill, passing a coast path post. Leave National Trust land via a gate. Keep on the coast path to rejoin the outward route (where the path left leads to Holdstone Down Cross). Keep ahead; at the next coast path sign turn left uphill for the car park. ●

If you keep going down the lane from point **C**, into **Trentishoe Combe,** you will reach the Hunter's Inn. The original thatched inn was burnt down in 1895, and was formerly popular with Oxford and Cambridge university students, visiting this part of the country on walking tours. The current building dates from 1897; look out for peacocks in the garden. But don't forget: it's a very long way back up to the route again...

? *What symbol is used to denote that you are on the South West Coast Path?*

Simonsbath

START Simonsbath
DISTANCE 3¾ miles (6km)
TIME 2 hours
PARKING Car park (charge) in Simonsbath
ROUTE FEATURES Boggy ground above Ashcombe Bottom on way to Prayway Head

10

This walk of great contrasts leads from the 'manufactured' 19th-century village of Simonsbath through Ashcombe Plantation up to wild open moorland and glorious views. The walk is peppered with reminders of the Knight family (see Walk 2), whose work on the moor in the 19th century led to the creation of the new parish of Exmoor, centred on Simonsbath.

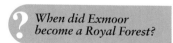 Walk to the upper car park; turn left up a footpath signed 'Prayway Head'. Climb steeply through the mature woodland of the Ashcombe Plantation, purchased by the Exmoor National Park Authority in 1978. The path levels off, then undulates through a more open area of oak, willow and cottongrass before dropping down and turning sharp left at a stock fence. Walk downhill, cross the stream, then go through a gate onto open grassland.

> **?** *When did Exmoor become a Royal Forest?*

A Follow the broad grassy path left round the hill. Pass a yellow-topped footpath pole, and another at the top of the field. Walk on to the top corner of the field and pass through a small wooden gate in the wall (yellow mark). Look back for lovely views of Birchcleave Woods (planted by the Knights in 1840) beyond Simonsbath. The Knights developed the village, building houses for miners working the copper and iron mines in the Barle Valley, as well as the church (St Luke Exmoor) in 1856, vicarage and school (which closed in 1970). Once through the gate the path becomes tussocky and boggy;

PUBLIC TRANSPORT None available
REFRESHMENTS Picnic area by car park; Boevey's Restaurant and Tearooms, Simonsbath House Hotel and Exmoor Forest Hotel in Simonsbath
PUBLIC TOILETS In car park
ORDNANCE SURVEY MAPS Explorer OL9 (Exmoor)

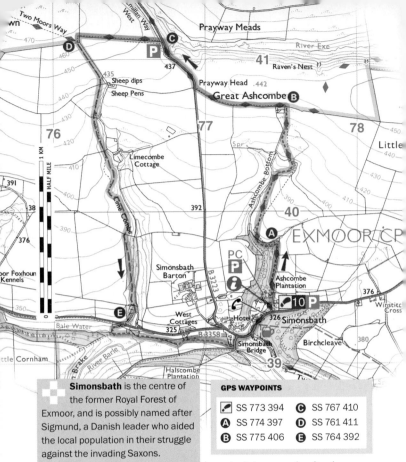

GPS WAYPOINTS

📍 SS 773 394	**C**	SS 767 410
A SS 774 397	**D**	SS 761 411
B SS 775 406	**E**	SS 764 392

Simonsbath is the centre of the former Royal Forest of Exmoor, and is possibly named after Sigmund, a Danish leader who aided the local population in their struggle against the invading Saxons.

follow the line of the bank on the right as the path runs over a small footbridge and curves left around a boggy area. Turn right by a post at the end of a stand of beech trees, then over a bank. The path becomes vague but is marked by odd yellow-topped posts; pick your way uphill across rough ground, keeping about 45 yds (50m) from the hedge on the left, to reach a five-bar gate in the wall ahead.

B Pass through the gate; turn left along the open moor, signed 'Prayway Head'. Walk on to meet the B3223 via a small gate; turn right and follow the verge; cross the road to reach the parking area at Prayway Head. Go through a small gate **C** and turn right signed 'bridleway to Exe Head' (the source of the River Exe lies 1,450ft [442m] above sea level on The Chains); then through the gate in the hedge and turn sharp left. At the end of that field note the signpost by the gate (straight on to Exe Head); look back for lovely views of Dunkery Beacon *(see Walk 6)*.

Pass through the gate, and turn left **D** through a metal gate in the next fence, signed 'bridleway to Simonsbath'. Walk downhill; it's wonderfully open and airy up here, with glorious views over the Barle valley. Pass through the next five-bar gate, with sheep pens left. Veer right (avoiding the boggy valley of Limecombe Bottom to your left), aiming for a single beech tree above the valley right. Go through the gap to the right of the tree and across the next field to a small gate in the hedgebank above Limecombe Cottage. Go straight ahead along the next field, keeping along the edge of the valley. This lovely, level, grassy route passes a blue-topped post; keep ahead eventually to pass another at the end of the field. Go through a five-bar gate in the hedgebank. Turn left, following sign 'bridleway through woods'. Follow blue-topped posts through a sycamore avenue above the combe. Turn left downhill at the end of the

Beechwoods overlooking the Barle near Simonsbath

wood, down a rough track and through a five-bar gate onto a track on a bend; keep ahead as signed to reach the B3358.

Turn left **E**, then right as signed on the footpath to Simonsbath. Pass through a gate, and immediately turn left on a narrow path. Follow the lovely signed path through woods and fields, over bridges and stiles, crossing the leat en route, eventually to cross it again just before the sawmill. Keep ahead through grassland to meet the road by Simonsbath Bridge. Turn left to meet the road opposite Simonsbath House Hotel (built by James Boevey in 1645 as a private house). Turn right on the road. Pass the Exmoor Forest Hotel (which used to own the River Barle from here to Pinkery Pond) on the left. Turn left for the car park. ●

11 *Withypool*

START Landacre Bridge

DISTANCE 4¼ miles (6.8km)

TIME 2¼ hours

PARKING In the higher of the two parking areas above Landacre Bridge

ROUTE FEATURES Steep narrow path uphill in Knighton Combe (boots off if stream is high); riverside path muddy in places; boggy ground on Withypool Common

Tucked away in the pretty Barle valley lies the sheltered village of Withypool, a place of some importance in the Royal Forest during medieval times, but today a peaceful village – popular with walkers and anglers – centred on Withypool Bridge. This varied walk leads along the Barle to the village centre before returning over the wilder open country of Withypool Common.

With your back to the river walk to the top of the grassy parking area. Turn left along a rough track, parallel to the river (below left). Cross the stream (ford) and follow the indistinct track ahead uphill, aiming for the top end of a line of beech trees ahead.

A At the signpost by the hedgebank, go straight on through the gate on the footpath signed 'Withypool'. Follow the hedgebank (left) to the end of the field; go through the right of two gates. At the end of that field pass over a stile by a gate. The path leads straight on

with a high hedgebank left. Pass a concrete shelter, and keep straight on between hedges. Turn left where signed up steps, over a stile and railed footbridge. Turn right and walk towards Brightworthy, an ancient farmstead dating back to the time of the Royal Forest; cross a

PUBLIC TRANSPORT Bus service from Taunton (Wednesday and Saturday only)

REFRESHMENTS Tearoom (seasonal) at Withypool Bridge; Royal Oak Inn in village; good picnic spot at Landacre Bridge

PUBLIC TOILETS In Withypool

ORDNANCE SURVEY MAPS Explorer OL9 (Exmoor)

stile, then follow signs left to pass the old millpond right. Go through a gate, and another by a stile. Walk straight across the field, downhill through a gap in the beech hedgebank, then right at the bottom signed 'Withypool' along the right bank of the Barle. The path from hereon follows the river, and is at times boggy, with footbridges and boardwalks. The path eventually runs a little away from the river, and crosses a stile to reach a green lane on a bend.

B The lane ahead is private; turn left over a stile into a meadow, and follow the path past the indoor

> **?** *Why are you asked to keep dogs under control when walking towards the green lane junction towards the end of point **A**?*

Withypool, named for the willows (withies) growing by the River Barle, was mentioned in the *Domesday Book*. It feels rather cut off today, surrounded by high open moorland, including the swell of Withypool Hill, which rises to a height of 1,306ft (398m) to the south. A Bronze Age stone circle can be found on its southern slopes, and a tumulus near its summit.

school at Waterhouse Farm (right), and over a stile. Keep ahead along the right edge to leave the field over a stile. Go through the gate and over the footbridge ahead; we have reached the edge of Withypool. Cross a small stile to reach six-arched Withypool Bridge, which is about 100 years old and replaced a medieval packhorse bridge, which lay a little upstream. Cross the bridge if you want refreshment at

GPS WAYPOINTS

⬛ SS 815 360	**C** SS 844 354
A SS 822 358	**D** SS 840 352
B SS 838 353	

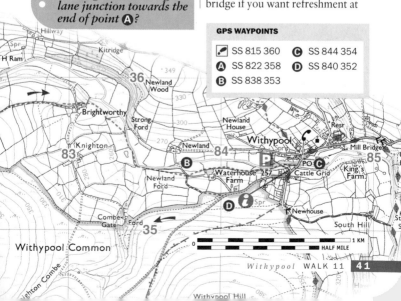

the pub (R.D. Blackmore, author of *Lorna Doone*, used to stay here) or to have a look at St Andrew's Church; it has a Norman font, and was heavily restored in the 19th century.

C Retrace your steps back over the bridge, cross the cattle-grid and keep straight on along the lane to pass the parking area (right). Turn first right opposite Hawthorne Bungalows, signed 'Sandy Way'. Follow the lane uphill to pass Waterhouse Farm (right).

D Take the next track on the right, which runs parallel to the lane at first, signed 'Landacre Bridge 2.' Where the track turns right into a field, keep straight on. The path narrows and drops steeply; follow it as it bears left above the stream in pretty Knighton Combe – a perfect

Withypool village

picnic spot. Cross the stream (you may have to remove boots). There's a steep climb up a deep narrow path on the other side onto open moorland. Follow the path across a concrete drive; the route continues along the edge of Withypool Common, with a big hedgebank on the right. The path is indistinct and boggy in places, but eventually follows the line of the hedgebank and drops downhill. Medieval five-arched Landacre Bridge can be seen in the valley ahead. In the days of the Royal Forest this was the site of the twice-yearly Forest Court (Swainmote), but today it is more likely to be host to great numbers of picnickers.

At the footpath post passed at point **A**, turn left and retrace your steps to your car. ●

You may see some **Exmoor ponies** on Withypool Common. These ponies, characterised by their stocky build, mealy-coloured muzzles and absence of any white markings, are all descended from ponies bought from Sir Thomas Dyke Acland by local farmers in 1818 when the Forest was sold by the Crown. The remaining pure-bred ponies both on and off the moor are carefully managed to maintain the breed's natural characteristics, essential to its survival.

Dulverton

START Marsh Bridge

DISTANCE 3¾ miles (6km)

TIME 2 hours

PARKING By the small footbridge near Marsh Bridge, off B3223 north of Dulverton

ROUTE FEATURES Long and steep climb at start of walk up Looseall Lane

12

A lovely walk that explores the peaceful woods, tracks and river valleys around the delightful little town of Dulverton, home to the headquarters of the Exmoor National Park Authority, and a popular, bustling centre for visitors to Exmoor. There's a really good National Park Information Centre here, too. Try to walk this one in May, when the bluebells are at their best.

Walk back to the B3223 via the little uphill 'link' lane. Cross the road and walk uphill under beech trees on the woodland track signed 'Court Down, Northcombe' (Loosehall Lane). This track is joined by another from the right; keep on steeply uphill to a T-junction of tracks, with a bench to the right.

A Turn left; pass through the gate onto open land, and turn right,

Who enabled the Exmoor National Park Authority to acquire part of Burridge Wood?

following the footpath sign. At the top of the hill pass through a small gate in the hedgebank on the right, and keep straight across the field to gain the trig point **B** on Court Down (1,037ft/316m). *Halfway to the trig point look right to find two gates in the hedgebank – the forward route.* Enjoy lovely views over Dulverton and the wooded valley of the Exe and Barle rivers. Turn right from the trig point and aim for the gates spotted on the way to it. Follow bridlepath signs for Dulverton through the gate on the left. Walk down the meadow, keeping the hedge right, and through a metal gate into the next

PUBLIC TRANSPORT Bus service from Minehead and Tiverton

REFRESHMENTS Range of pubs and cafés in Dulverton; Lewis's Tearooms

PUBLIC TOILETS In car park in Dulverton

ORDNANCE SURVEY MAPS Explorer OL9 (Exmoor)

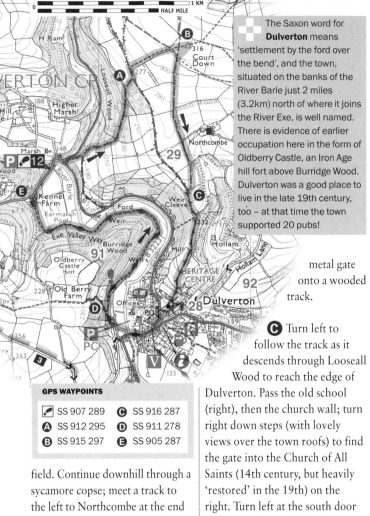

The Saxon word for **Dulverton** means 'settlement by the ford over the bend', and the town, situated on the banks of the River Barle just 2 miles (3.2km) north of where it joins the River Exe, is well named. There is evidence of earlier occupation here in the form of Oldberry Castle, an Iron Age hill fort above Burridge Wood. Dulverton was a good place to live in the late 19th century, too – at that time the town supported 20 pubs!

metal gate onto a wooded track.

C Turn left to follow the track as it descends through Looseall Wood to reach the edge of Dulverton. Pass the old school (right), then the church wall; turn right down steps (with lovely views over the town roofs) to find the gate into the Church of All Saints (14th century, but heavily 'restored' in the 19th) on the right. Turn left at the south door and leave the church via the lychgate; walk straight on through Bank Square, then into Fore Street, passing the Town Hall on the left – made famous by its frequent appearances in the film

GPS WAYPOINTS

SS 907 289	**C** SS 916 287
A SS 912 295	**D** SS 911 278
B SS 915 297	**E** SS 905 287

field. Continue downhill through a sycamore copse; meet a track to the left to Northcombe at the end of the field, and go through the small gate ahead. At the end of the next field pass a solitary gatepost, and continue downhill, aiming for a huge tree on a bank. Just past the tree turn sharp right through a

Cottages by the River Barle below Dunster Bridge

The Land Girls – then down the High Street. Keep on over a small bridge; note the plaque on the wall here marking the height of the River Barle at the time of the Lynmouth flood in August 1952 *(see Walk 17)* – it was incredibly high. Pass the office of the Exmoor National Park Authority

There's a good chance that you'll see a dipper as you walk along the banks of the **Barle**. This charismatic yet solitary little bird, easily identified by its white throat and breast, and chestnut underparts, has the ability to walk and swim underwater in fast-flowing streams as it searches for food. If you do this walk during the spring you'll also enjoy delicate wood anemones, strong-smelling ramsons – evidence of old, undisturbed woodland – and bluebells.

on the right, and cross the bridge over the Barle.

D Turn immediately right along a small lane. Where the lane bears left keep ahead up a dead end lane, steeply uphill to pass a small well (left); follow footpath signs right along a deeply banked lane. Keep straight on, signed 'Tarr Steps and Hawkridge'. Keep on the track as it undulates through Burridge Wood above the River Barle below right. The path drops down towards the river and curves left to follow its course, then becomes narrow and rocky, with one steep stepped section. Bear right at the next junction, following signs for Marsh Bridge. Pass a beautiful house (left), then go through two wooden gates to meet the road **E**. Turn right downhill, following signs for Tarr Steps, to pass Kennel Farm on the right. Cross Marsh Bridge (former site of a 19th-century mock Gothic chapel, which burnt down in 1900), then turn right over the old footbridge to find your car.

13 *Horner Wood*

START The western edge of Ley Hill, west of Horner valley/Wood

DISTANCE 4¼ miles (6.8km)

TIME 2½ hours

PARKING On open ground (unmarked) opposite entrance to Lucott Farm

ROUTE FEATURES Steep descent down Halse Combe to Horner; some paths muddy after wet weather

Most walks through Horner Wood start from the car park in Horner. This one however, does something different (and avoids the crowds) by starting high above the Horner Valley, making the most of the fantastic views. Midway, you can have a break in one of the tea gardens at Horner before walking back through the ancient oak woodlands.

From the parking area follow the track away from the road; keep on it as it turns sharp left to run along the side of the hill high above the wooded valley below, with stunning views towards the Vale of Porlock and the sea. Horner Wood is part of the Dunkery and Horner Wood National Nature Reserve and lies within the extensive Holnicote Estate *(see Walk 20)*; covering more than 800 acres (331 hectares) it is the largest area of ancient oak woodland in the British Isles, with ash in the valley bottoms. Follow the track until it bends very sharply to the left towards the road, at a junction of unmarked paths.

Ⓐ Turn right down a broad grassy path. At the first crossroads of paths turn left, with superb views of Halse Combe and Bossington Hill beyond. Pass monumental stone Pentley Seat on the left, in memory of Charles Thomas Dyke Acland and his wife Gertrude, who died in 1919 and 1920 respectively.

Stoke Pero church, situated on the edge of Horner Wood and Stoke Pero Common, is well worth a visit. Set 1,013ft (309m) above sea level, it has a fantastically peaceful setting. The tower and porch are possibly 12th century, but the present building dates from 1897. The population of the parish numbered 100 in 1790, but has dropped well below that today.

PUBLIC TRANSPORT None available

REFRESHMENTS Horner Vale Tea Gardens and Horner Tea Garden

PUBLIC TOILETS In car park at Horner

ORDNANCE SURVEY MAPS Explorer OL9 (Exmoor)

At the next T-junction of paths (Granny's Ride) turn left **B**. The path drops gradually to another junction. Turn right downhill, signed Horner. Follow the path steeply and carefully down the edge of Halse Combe (dropping sharply away left) through oaks and birches to meet a woodland track, with a campsite through the hedge opposite.

C Turn right along the track through a gate bearing a Coleridge Way symbol (quill). Eventually follow the track left over an old packhorse bridge to meet the lane. Turn left for the car park and toilets; turn right for the tearooms at Horner Green. It's worth taking a moment to have a look at the picturesque cottages and mill; interestingly the name 'Horner' is thought to derive from the Saxon *hwrnwr* – 'snorer' – after the rushing waters of the Horner Water.

D To continue, walk south from Horner Green on the track leading into the woods (Horner Water right). Cross the river on a stone

GPS WAYPOINTS

🔖 SS 880 447	**D** SS 897 454
A SS 890 452	**E** SS 896 438
B SS 895 454	**F** SS 890 439
C SS 897 458	

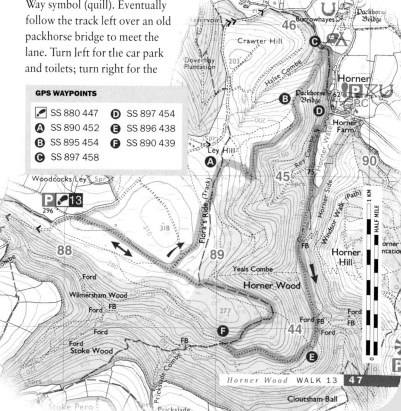

View towards Bossington Hill

You have to go through a gate into Horner Wood during point **C** of the walk. What would you do if you had to unlock it?

clearing; Pool Bridge is signed straight ahead.

E Bear right uphill on a broad path (ignore tiny Stags Path, soon passed on the right). This delightful path climbs through beautiful light oak woodland to another junction of paths. Much of the oak woodland here was coppiced to produce bark for the tanning industry, and there are references relating to this activity in Horner Wood as far back as 1572. There is also evidence of charcoal burning and, at the top edge of the woods, an Iron Age enclosure and the remains of a deserted settlement thought to date from late Anglo-Saxon or early Medieval times.

bridge, then turn left on the main track through a gate. Walk on; the river, now to the left, is extremely pretty here; there are several good picnic spots beneath the trees near the water's edge. Pass two wooden footbridges, the second of which is signed to Dunkery Beacon. The track runs uphill to a grassy

F Turn right on Granny's Ride (bridlepath); follow this narrow path uphill. At the next junction bear left to leave Granny's Ride, signed Ley Hill and Horner Gate. At the top edge of the woods a bridlepath (Flora's Ride) runs away right. Ignore this and keep straight on to meet the outward track on a bend. Keep straight on and retrace your steps to your car. ●

Horner Wood is an SSSI, and home to a great variety of plant and animal species, including more than 200 species of lichen. Red deer (the British Isles' largest native land animal) shelter in the woodland when the weather is bad higher up on the open moor. The National Trust's policy of leaving dead and decaying timber provides ideal habitats for various beetles and a great variety of fungi; the wood supports more than 400 species, 20 per cent of which are considered rare.

Winsford

START Winsford
DISTANCE 3¾ miles (6km)
TIME 2 hours
PARKING Car park (free) in centre of Winsford
ROUTE FEATURES Steep climb from Withycombe Farm to the top of The Punchbowl

14

Winsford, with its pretty thatched cottages, flower-filled gardens, bridges and streams, is a delightful spot. This walk of great contrasts leads from the village through farmland to the wilder moorland and spectacular scenery around The Punchbowl – thought to have been created by the Devil – on the edge of Winsford Hill.

Walk from the car park back to the junction of lanes by the bridge in the middle of the village. Apart from its reputation as one of the most picturesque villages on Exmoor, Winsford's other claim to fame is that the eminent Labour politician Ernest Bevin was born here in 1881.

A Turn right; follow the lane past the war memorial (left) and cross the Winn Brook via the footbridge by the ford. Walk up Ash Lane,

> **?** What will happen if you are seen dropping litter in the middle of Winsford?

passing the medieval Church of St Mary Magdalene above right. The lane climbs steadily uphill.

B Where the lane bends right, turn left through a gate signed 'footpath to Winsford Hill'; then right over a stile onto a narrow fenced path. Follow this over a stile into a field, then over another stile onto a narrow path, then through a kissing-gate into open fields. Walk straight on along the bottom of the field. Go through a metal gate in the next hedge, and along the next field, with the pretty valley of the Winn Brook and the steep slope of Burrow Wood left. Pass through the right of two five-bar gates in

---

PUBLIC TRANSPORT Bus service from Dulverton and Minehead (not Sunday)
REFRESHMENTS Royal Oak Inn and Bridge Cottage Tearooms (seasonal) in Winsford
PUBLIC TOILETS By Winsford village hall, near parking area
ORDNANCE SURVEY MAPS Explorer OL9 (Exmoor)

the next hedge, under a big ash tree. Walk through the field, then a kissing-gate, then through a gate at the end of the next field. Pass a small ruined building (left). Pass through a gate in the next hedgebank, and straight over the next field, aiming for the right (uphill) of two gates (a notice by the lower gate indicates that the path has been diverted). Go through the gate and walk on to join the drive leading to Withycombe Farm.

C Turn left down the drive and through a gate on the bridlepath. Look over the farm buildings to see the spectacular natural feature of The Punchbowl, which lies just below Winsford Hill. Where the drive turns into the farmyard (left), keep straight on to pass a big metal barn (right). Follow the concrete

way downhill through a gate to cross the Winn Brook, then uphill. At the entrance to Withycombe Cottage (unsigned) follow the track right uphill. You will meet two big gates; go through the one on the left, and turn right to follow the ridge running uphill. This is quite a steep climb: take the time to enjoy the views back down the valley to Winsford which unfold with every step. Where the path levels out a little, turn right where signed through a gate, then left uphill to follow a lovely line of beeches. Pass through a gate onto open moorland on the edge of Winsford Hill (NT). Follow the broad grassy path uphill; after 100 yds (91m) keep left when the path forks **D**. The path curves left round the top of The Punchbowl, which drops very steeply away left: it's about 650ft (200m) down to the valley floor. Keep left, ignoring all other paths. The path then runs a little away from the edge, through heather and gorse – you may well see Exmoor ponies, members of the Anchor herd, descendants of Sir Thomas Acland's ponies (*see Walk 11*). Keep

Under a shelter near Spire Cross on Winsford Hill can be found the famous **Caratacus stone**. Inscribed with the words 'Caratacus Nepus', it is the only inscribed stone from the Dark Ages to have been found in Somerset, and is thought to commemorate a relative/kinsman of the British king Caratacus, who led a resistance against the Romans. The stone dates from the 5th or 6th century. The shelter was built in 1906, but the stone has since been vandalised; it was re-erected in 1937, but accounts of its recent history vary.

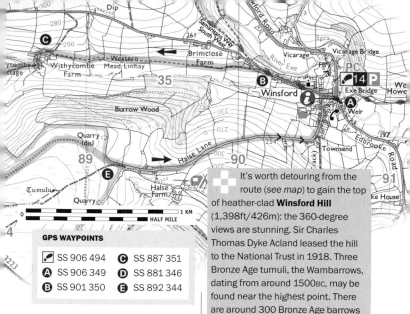

GPS WAYPOINTS

📷 SS 906 494	**C** SS 887 351
A SS 906 349	**D** SS 881 346
B SS 901 350	**E** SS 892 344

It's worth detouring from the route (*see map*) to gain the top of heather-clad **Winsford Hill** (1,398ft/426m): the 360-degree views are stunning. Sir Charles Thomas Dyke Acland leased the hill to the National Trust in 1918. Three Bronze Age tumuli, the Wambarrows, dating from around 1500BC, may be found near the highest point. There are around 300 Bronze Age barrows on Exmoor.

on the path, which runs gently downhill to meet the lane opposite Halse Farm.

E Turn left through the gate by the cattle-grid and follow the lane downhill to Winsford. Pass the thatched Royal Oak Inn on the right; look left to see the pretty old stone packhorse bridge over the Winn Brook. Winsford is blessed with eight varied bridges! Walk on past the war memorial (left) to return to your car. ●

Hawthorn tree above The Punchbowl, looking towards Dunkery Beacon

15 *Bury and Wimbleball Lake*

START Bury
DISTANCE 4½ miles (7.2km)
TIME 2½ hours
PARKING On the lane in the centre of Bury, near the phone box
ROUTE FEATURES Early part of Haddon Lane from Bury towards Haddon Farm steep and sometimes muddy

Tucked away just to the east of the Exe valley near Dulverton lies the little village of Bury, where time seems to have stood still. This lovely walk leads over the top of heather-and-gorse-covered Hadborough, rising to 1,165ft (355m) on Haddon Hill, then down to the edge of Wimbleball Lake before following an easy return route along the pretty valley of the River Haddeo.

Parking is not easy in Bury, but you should be able to tuck your car away on the left of the lane going towards the phone box.

Walk past the phone box. About 10 yds (9m) beyond it turn right **A**, following a small overgrown bridleway sign up a tarmac track to pass Pixton Barn (left) and Virginia Cottage (right). Go through the gate ahead and up the deeply banked, frequently muddy Haddon Lane. The track passes through a wooden gate to enter an oak glade, with lovely views over the deep wooded Haddeo valley to the left.

Brompton Regis church

Pass through another gate, along a green lane, and through a gate at Haddon Farm. Follow bridleway

PUBLIC TRANSPORT Bus service from Dulverton (Thursdays only))
REFRESHMENTS None on route; the George Inn in Brompton Regis
PUBLIC TOILETS None on route
ORDNANCE SURVEY MAPS Explorer OL9 (Exmoor)

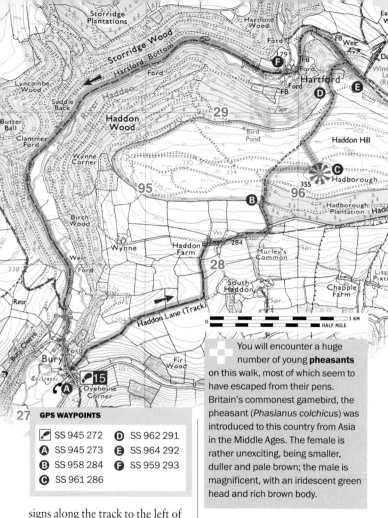

GPS WAYPOINTS

📍 SS 945 272	Ⓓ SS 962 291
Ⓐ SS 945 273	Ⓔ SS 964 292
Ⓑ SS 958 284	Ⓕ SS 959 293
Ⓒ SS 961 286	

You will encounter a huge number of young **pheasants** on this walk, most of which seem to have escaped from their pens. Britain's commonest gamebird, the pheasant (*Phasianus colchicus*) was introduced to this country from Asia in the Middle Ages. The female is rather unexciting, being smaller, duller and pale brown; the male is magnificent, with an iridescent green head and rich brown body.

signs along the track to the left of the farm. The track curves uphill to enter a beechwood; about 20 yds (18m) into the wood turn left over a stile in the wire fence. Ignore the footpath sign and turn left along the inside of the fence, then right uphill at the corner of the wood.

At the top pass through a gate Ⓑ onto open heath on the edge of Haddon Hill. Follow the track

? *Who has a track named after her on this walk?*

Cottage garden in Bury, late summer

right along the edge of the old Hadborough Plantation.

Where the track bends 90 degrees right on the corner, bear half left on a broad track across the heather and gorse. At the next major track turn right and walk towards the highest point of Haddon Hill, Hadborough.

From the trig point **C** return to the track and take the left of two narrow paths ahead downhill, heading towards the wooded valley below. Meet a track and turn right downhill towards the lake. When level with the dam turn left. Pick your way downhill, eventually bearing left to meet a track. Turn right towards the dam, then left **D**

down a little path (look carefully for the footpath sign to Hartford), over a stile, then downhill through beautiful oak and birch woodland, passing a multitude of pheasants en route. The path ends down steep steps to hit a concrete lane; *turn right uphill to go and have a look at the reservoir dam* **E**, *an impressive sight at 975ft (300m) long and 218ft (67m) high. Wimbleball was completed in the late 1970s, and holds 4,740 million gallons (21,500 megalitres) of water, much of which feeds into the Haddeo for extraction at Tiverton and Exeter.*

Retrace your steps down the concrete lane. Where a branch goes right over the stream keep straight on, with the stream right. Pass through a gate by a cattle-grid into a field; turn left off the concrete way, signed 'bridlepath', along a grassy path between post-and-rail fencing. Pass through a wooden gate, then right over a footbridge over the river. Follow the path left, then right to pass through the grounds of Hartford Mill, then straight on to meet a track with Haddon Springs Trout Hatchery left. Walk to the T-junction of tracks.

F Turn left, signed 'Bury'. The track passes through a gate, then runs gently along the Haddeo Valley: it's a really lovely, level route through the Pixton Estate, with lots of picnic and paddling opportunities. Lady Harriet Acland lived at Pixton in the 18th and

Bury is a beautiful spot, with some delightful cottages and gardens. Its name means 'fortified place'; Bury Castle, the remains of a Norman motte-and-bailey, lie tucked away in private woodland just west of the centre. The ford and narrow bridge over the River Haddeo, a tributary of the Exe, prevents much through traffic. This was once a rural community, as evidenced by the old school, old forge, old chapel and old church, all now converted into houses.

early 19th centuries. Pass two white cottages below left; continue on to pass through a gate by Bury Lodge, then pass Hunts Farm, to reach the village of Bury. Turn left to cross the river by the ford on the picturesque medieval four-arched bridge, and follow the lane back to your car. ●

Looking towards Wimbleball Lake from Haddon Hill

16 *Luxborough*

START Kingsbridge, Luxborough

DISTANCE 3½ miles (5.6km)

TIME 2 hours

PARKING Car park (contributions cairn for Luxborough Village Field charity) at Kingsbridge

ROUTE FEATURES Long ascent from Churchtown to Withycombe Hill

The isolated village of Luxborough, tucked away within the folds of the rolling Brendon Hills of eastern Exmoor, is made up of three distinct hamlets – Churchtown, Kingsbridge, and Pooltown – and this walk visits all three. This route leads to the top of Withycombe Common, where there are superb far-reaching views, from Dunkery Beacon in the west to the Quantock Hills in the east.

Turn right out of the car park, and walk up the lane to pass Luxborough Village Hall, playground and public field on the right. Cross the bridge over the Washford river at Pooltown.

Iron ore was mined in the **Brendon Hills** in Roman times; the Roman lode runs from here to Simonsbath. In 1856 the West Somerset Mineral Railway was built from the top of Brendon Hill (southeast of Luxborough) and west to Goosemoor, with a link to the coast at Watchet via a 1 in 4 incline at Comberow. By the late 19th century cheaper ore from elsewhere heralded the end of mining activity. The last remaining engine house can be seen at Burrow Farm, south of the B3224.

A Immediately over the bridge, turn right through low wooden posts to walk across a small grassy area and then along a little wooded path that undulates above the river. Follow the path as it bears left to follow a tributary stream, which runs by the path on the right, with fields beyond. The path becomes more track-like and passes a

 What must you not do in the village field?

PUBLIC TRANSPORT Bus service from Taunton (Wednesday and Saturday only)

REFRESHMENTS Royal Oak Inn at Kingsbridge, tea garden (seasonal) at Pooltown

PUBLIC TOILETS None on route

PLAY AREA Near the village hall, Kingsbridge

ORDNANCE SURVEY MAPS Explorer OL9 (Exmoor)

Church of St Mary at Churchtown

sandstone house below right; 20 yds (18m) farther on, where the track rises up left, keep straight along the path through an area of tall scattered conifers. The path joins a gritty lane near Thorney Cottage (below right).

Walk uphill to meet the lane. Look right over the hedge for views of the church tower at Churchtown. Turn right **B** and walk downhill, then steeply uphill to meet another lane on a bend at Butcher's Farm. Walk straight on, left round the corner, then right to have a look at the Church of St Mary, part of which dates from the 13th century, and which has an interesting saddleback tower. Although the present tower dates from 1861, records show that the church tower

always had this type of roof. The building, apart from the tower and porch, has been limewashed in the traditional manner (*see Walk 4*). It is possible that the shaft of the old stone cross in the churchyard dates from Saxon times, making it the oldest on Exmoor.

From the church turn right uphill to find West Cott Cottages (left), and Vine Cottage (right). Turn right **C**, signed 'bridleway to Croydon Hill'. The path passes through a gate leading between a white cottage and barn, then through a gate into a field (unsigned). Note the old earthwork mound to the left here. Walk up the field and through the right of two gates; continue up the broad grassy swathe to meet a gate by a

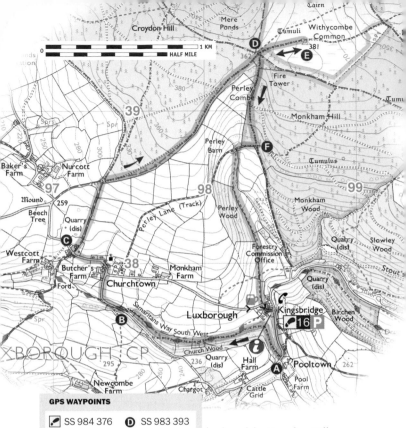

GPS WAYPOINTS

✏ SS 984 376	**D** SS 983 393
A SS 985 373	**E** SS 986 394
B SS 974 377	**F** SS 983 387
C SS 971 381	

bench at the top. Pause for a breather, and look back for lovely views towards Kennisham Hill. Pass through the gate and follow the grassy path to its end; bear left, then right on a forest track. Meet another on a bend; keep straight on, signed 'bridleway to Dunster'. This track climbs steadily along the edge of the Croydon Hill coniferous plantation to reach a junction of tracks.

D Take the footpath straight ahead, signed 'Rodhuish', to gain the trig point **E** and earthwork enclosure on Withycombe Common (1,250ft/381m) with its fabulous views. Return to the path junction **D**; walk across the track and down the bridlepath to Luxborough (immediately to the

View over Kingsbridge

through another gate, and then another to hit the lane at the edge of Kingsbridge. Walk downhill to pass the 17th-century Royal Oak Inn on the left. The oldest part, at the back, dates from 1375. Cross the bridge opposite one of Luxborough's unusual round houses: designed by John Crispin, there are seven of these around the parish, marking the boundary of the Chargot Estate. Mostly built as two cottages, they are known locally as the 'pregnant cottages' on account of their unusual 'bulge', which originally accommodated two spiral staircases. Turn right for the car park. ●

left of the one on which you arrived from Churchtown). Follow this steeply downhill through a coniferous plantation. The path curves away from the fields (right).

At the end of the trees on the right turn right **F** on a clear track that runs along the top of Perley Combe. Pass through the gate at the end of the track; turn left through another gate and walk downhill, aiming for a gate in the bottom right corner on the edge of Perley Wood. Keep going along the edge of the wood, and through another gate. Keep on downhill

An interesting find was made near the east end of the church during restoration work in 1996. The remains of 12 unknown individuals, probably dating from the 12th to 14th centuries, were discovered, and were reburied close by on Mothering Sunday 1998. There is also a fantastic millennium stained-glass window in the church, created by a local craftsman. The new window has been fixed in the same position as an old one that was discovered during dry rot and damp repairs.

17 *Watersmeet*

START Combe Park, Hillsford Bridge
DISTANCE 5 miles (8km)
TIME 2¾ hours
PARKING Car park at Combe Park (donation box)
ROUTE FEATURES Steep sometimes slippery descent on Two Moors Way from Oxen Tor

The Lynmouth area is well known for the devastating floods that took place here in August 1952. This spectacular walk, which starts high above the deep valleys of the East Lyn and Hoaorak rivers, gives an insight into the landscape features that exacerbated the disaster. The return route through ancient oak woodland criss-crosses the sparkling river and brings with it the prospect of refreshments in the garden at Watersmeet House.

Leave the car park; turn left to meet the main road by Hillsford Bridge. Turn left and walk uphill. On the first bend take the path right, signed 'East Lyn and Lynmouth' (on the Two Moors Way) to enter the Watersmeet Estate, owned by the National Trust. The estate covers 2,000 acres (800ha) of beautiful countryside, much of it a designated SSSI: rocky cliffs, steep oak-wooded valleys, open heathland and rushing rivers. There are also 38 miles (61km) of footpaths, including part of the Two Moors Way: this long-distance footpath runs for 102 miles

The National Trust's **Watersmeet House** (café and shop) occupies a delightful situation at the junction of the two rivers. In the late 18th century places such as Lynmouth and Watersmeet started to become fashionable as a result of the Romantic Movement, and the site was bought by Rev W.S. Halliday in 1829. He built the house as a retreat and hunting lodge in 1932. A huge old Monterey pine graces its pretty garden; a younger replacement has already been planted.

(163km) from Ivybridge in south Devon, over Dartmoor and Exmoor, to reach the north coast at Lynmouth.

PUBLIC TRANSPORT Seasonal bus service from Ilfracombe and Minehead
REFRESHMENTS Range of pubs and cafés in Lynmouth; also NT café at Watersmeet (seasonal)
PUBLIC TOILETS At Watersmeet, and in Lynmouth (off route)
ORDNANCE SURVEY MAPS Explorer OL9 (Exmoor)

A Ascend through light woodland to more open country with Myrtleberry South Iron Age camp off the path to the left. The broad grassy path now runs along the top of the oak woodlands in the valley of the Hoaroak Water, below right. As you continue along the path the complicated pattern of valleys and hills becomes clear: you can see the junction of the steep-sided and thickly wooded East Lyn and Hoaroak valleys, with the broad swell of Countisbury Common above, rising to 1,125ft (343m). The East Lyn has cut deeply into the moorland plateau, and runs 600ft (200m) below; the landscape here is quite dramatic. Ignore a path to Watersmeet (right) to reach a post at Myrtleberry Cleave **B**, with wonderful views towards the sea.

Continue on the path through two small gates. The path bends sharp right to pass a stone seat, then zigzags steeply and stonily downhill to cross a waterfall, then uphill to pass a path to West Lyn and Barbrook. At the signpost for Oxen Tor **C** follow the Two Moors Way sign right and steeply down through woodland eventually to leave the Watersmeet Estate. The zigag path meets houses at the edge of Lynmouth and becomes tarmac: *take care – it can be very slippery here*. The path reaches Watersmeet Road **D** opposite the Anglican church, by an engraved stone that commemorates the opening of the Two Moors Way on 29 April 1976. Turn left.
To take a look at Lynmouth keep straight ahead.

Watersmeet House, at the confluence of the East Lyn and Hoaroak rivers

Wild garlic by the waterfall on the Hoaroak Water

To continue the walk, turn right through the car park towards the river. Turn right along the riverside path and walk upstream. Ignore the first white-railed footbridge over the river. Where the Victorian houses on the opposite bank come to an end, look out for a notice by the path stating that this is the site of Middleham, where 10 houses were destroyed in the floods. Cross the next wooden footbridge (Woodside Bridge); turn right and continue upriver on the left bank. A plaque on the right commemorates the handing over of the Watersmeet Estate to the National Trust in 1936. Follow the riverside path as signed; after a while it rises uphill away from the river. At the next junction (Woodland Walk left fork) take the right fork (Watersmeet Riverside Walk). Descend to cross the river on wooden Blackpool Bridge, then later cross back again to the left bank over Lynrock Bridge **E** (unsigned). (The path straight ahead here – on the right bank – crosses the site of an old mineral water factory.) Having crossed the bridge turn right – even though the path is signed to Lynmouth – and zigzag uphill to join a larger path at a T-junction. Turn right on the Woodland Walk.

The path runs high above the river and the house at Myrtleberry before dropping down to Chiselcombe Bridge, opened in 1957, and built as a result of public subscription after an earlier bridge

On the night of 15 August 1952, at the height of the holiday season, a 40ft (12m) wall of water, boulders and debris surged down the valley, destroying everything – bridges, houses, cars – in its path. Thirty-four people – one of whom was never identified – lost their lives, The flood resulted from a build-up of water on **The Chains** (see *Walk 2*): 9in (228m) of rainwater fell in 24 hours, one of the heaviest periods of rainfall ever recorded in the British Isles.

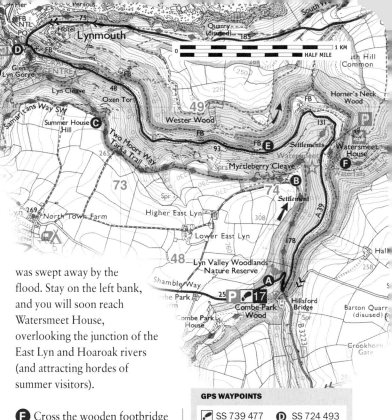

was swept away by the flood. Stay on the left bank, and you will soon reach Watersmeet House, overlooking the junction of the East Lyn and Hoaroak rivers (and attracting hordes of summer visitors).

F Cross the wooden footbridge over the East Lyn, above the meeting point of the two rivers; turn right, then go left up steep steps, signed 'Hillsford Bridge'. Turn right and follow the woodland path uphill with the Hoaroak Water below left. The woodland floor here is carpeted with heady ramsons – wild garlic – in May. Pass the waterfall – *it's worth branching off the route to have a closer look* – and continue uphill to leave the estate at

Hillsford Bridge. Turn right, cross the bridge, then left and first right into the car park. ●

GPS WAYPOINTS

✏ SS 739 477	**D** SS 724 493
A SS 740 479	**E** SS 738 487
B SS 741 485	**F** SS 744 486
C SS 728 489	

> **?** Somewhere on the walk you will come across an area known as The Cleaves. Who gave this to the National Trust, and when?

18 *Culbone*

START Porlock Weir	
DISTANCE 5½ miles (8.8km)	
TIME 3 hours	
PARKING Car park (fee paying) at Porlock Weir	
ROUTE FEATURES Undulating coast path, sometimes steep and muddy; long climb from Culbone up Withy Combe	

A long walk of great contrasts – and some steep ascents – starting from the characterful harbour at Porlock Weir at the west end of the broad sweep of Porlock Bay, and leading through the woods to the secluded little church at Culbone, with its tales of lepers and charcoal burners, before returning via quiet lanes across wide open farmland and pretty light oak woodland.

Tranquil Porlock Weir was a working and fishing harbour until the early 20th century. Coal, limestone and cement were brought in from south Wales, and agricultural produce (from the Vale of Porlock), tan bark, charcoal and pitprops (from the neighbouring woodland) were shipped out. Today it attracts sightseers, coast path walkers and pleasure craft. Walk out of the car park and ahead between the Anchor Hotel and the Ship Inn on the coast path, signed 'Culbone'. Follow the path behind the hotel and through a gate along the bottom of a field, and through another gate. The path runs away from the sea uphill through a five-bar gate, then another, to meet the lane near a farm (right).

> **Porlock Hill** was the scene of an incredible feat of strength and determination on a stormy night in January 1899. Due to the dreadful weather the Lynmouth lifeboat, *Louisa*, could not be launched; a team of men and 18 horses spent the night dragging her 10 miles (16km) up over Countisbury (with a gradient of 1:4) and down Porlock Hill. She was launched from Porlock Weir and went to the assistance of the *Forest Hall*, a three-masted schooner, which was eventually towed by tug to Barry in south Wales.

PUBLIC TRANSPORT Bus service from Minehead
REFRESHMENTS Anchor Hotel, Ship Inn and tearooms at Porlock Weir
PUBLIC TOILETS In car park
ORDNANCE SURVEY MAPS Explorer OL9 (Exmoor)

Church of St Beuno, Culbone, seen from the coast path

A Turn right along the lane, passing Worthy Manor (right) to reach the arched thatched tollgate at Worthy Combe (private). In 1866 Lord Lovelace had an Italianate-style mansion – Ashley Combe House – built nearby; although the house has been demolished, there is evidence of various garden terraces and tunnels along the path. The footpath leaves the lane right and runs steeply uphill under a tunnel through dark woods before zigzagging (some steps) uphill. The path levels off then drops down steps and continues to undulate, with some steep sections, until it turns inland towards Culbone Combe, to reach the little church (below right).

Cross the stream on a stone bridge with the house on the left, then turn right **B** to leave the coast path and right into the churchyard. Culbone church is only accessible on foot. This is a wonderfully peaceful spot, with little sound other than birdsong and the babbling of the stream. During the 13th to 18th centuries there were colonies of lepers living in these remote woods, making their living from cutting timbers and tan bark and producing charcoal. It is said that at one time lepers outnumbered the local deer population.

Culbone's pretty little **Church of St Beuno** is the smallest complete parish church in England, measuring a mere 35ft (10.5m) in length. Named for a 6th-century Welsh saint, it dates from the late 12th century, although it is possible that parts of the building are Saxon (early 11th century). A tiny slit in the north wall is known as the 'leper's window'; some believe that local lepers, excluded from contact with other people, managed to get a view of the altar here, but this is unproven. This remote, sparsely populated parish was combined with that of Oare (see *Walk 4*) in 1933.

From the church door walk ahead to the top left corner of the churchyard and exit via a small gate. Turn left uphill, signed County Gate and Silcombe Farm, following the stream up Withy (the old name for willow) Combe, signed 'County Gate'. The path passes under the coast path by the cottage (right), then climbs steeply uphill. Follow it sharp right away from the stream through a wooden gate under sycamores. A T-junction of tracks is reached at the end of the wood; turn left uphill to rejoin the coast path. The track climbs steeply and passes through a gate, with great views of Hurlstone Point behind; it's a relief to be out in the breezy open countryside. The track meets a lane through a wooden gate at the top of the hill, with Silcombe Farm ahead and right.

C Turn left along the peaceful lane, which undulates pleasantly past Culbone Parsonage between banks of wildflowers – greater stitchwort, red campion, vetches, foxgloves, cow parsley, pennywort, speedwell and buttercups – it's

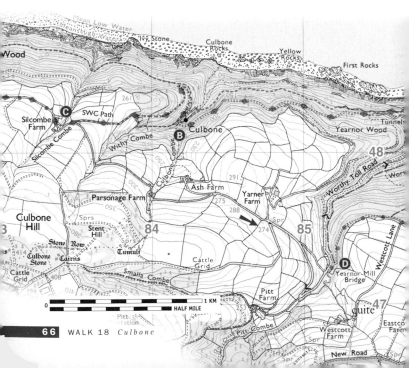

? *What is unusual about the chimneys at Culbone Parsonage?*

beautiful. Look right up to the great swell of Porlock Common, rising to 1,431ft (436m), and over which runs the notoriously steep A39. Pass the drive to Ash Farm on the left; it has been suggested that Samuel Taylor Coleridge was staying here when he wrote the incomplete *Kubla Khan*. Just past the drive to Yarner Farm, you hit a lane on a sharp bend. Walk straight on, signed 'Porlock Weir via Worthy Toll Road'. Follow the lane downhill to where it turns sharp left (lane right to Pitt Farm only). Keep on downhill to the edge of Worthy Wood.

D Turn right through a gate into the wood, on a path signed 'Porlock Weir'. The toll road runs downhill, marked 'Private toll road: no walkers or horses'. A few yards into the wood ignore the bridleway sign left; keep straight ahead on the footpath (red markers) for 'Porlock Wier' [sic]. This lovely broad path, a mass of bluebells in spring, runs along the top edge of the woods. Where a bridlepath leaves the track left, keep straight on signed 'Porlockford'. The path continues downhill and becomes roughly tarmacked at the next junction of paths; keep straight on for Porlock Weir. Proceed carefully downhill to meet a T-junction of tracks **E**.

Turn left and follow the track round the hill. Where it bends sharp right, keep ahead on a bridlepath signed to Yearnor Mill Lane. After 50 yds (46m) bear right on a narrow path, which zigzags downhill through woodland to meet a lane. Turn right, then take the first lane left to reach the car park.

GPS WAYPOINTS	
✏ SS 864 478	**C** SS 835 481
A SS 859 481	**D** SS 851 472
B SS 841 481	**E** SS 863 473

19 *Exford*

START Exford
DISTANCE 5½ miles (8.8km)
TIME 3 hours
PARKING Exford car park (free)
ROUTE FEATURES Some paths frequently muddy, especially those close to the river in the middle of the walk; long steep climb up Room Hill from river

A long but rewarding walk that starts from Exford, situated in the very heart of Exmoor at an ancient crossing of the Exe, Exmoor's longest river, and leads along the beautiful wooded Exe valley, before returning over Room and Road Hills. The tough climb up the valley side onto the top of Room Hill is rewarded with great views over the typical patchwork of fields and hedges so characteristic of this part of Exmoor.

✏ Walk away from the village centre and through the kissing-gate at the end of the car park. Follow the track through another kissing-gate, along the route of the Exe Valley Way, to pass Gulley Pool on the right. Pass through the kissing-gate by the bridge opposite Court Farm.

🅐 Turn left, signed 'Higher Combe and Lyncombe'. The track leads uphill away from the river, passing a footpath to the church (left). The Church of St Mary Magdalene dates from the mid 15th century, but was heavily

Exford has long been known as the great hunting centre of Exmoor; there seem to be horses everywhere, and both pubs are full of hunting memorabilia. The kennels and stables of the Devon and Somerset Staghounds were moved here in 1875, and Exford became a popular centre for huntsmen, fishermen and tourists. At one time there were four blacksmiths' forges in operation.

restored in the 19th; earlier buildings on this site, dating to pre-Norman times, were dedicated to the Celtic saint Salvyn. It also has a 15th-century screen with an unusual story: the village bought it

PUBLIC TRANSPORT Bus service from Minehead, Tiverton and Taunton
REFRESHMENTS Crown Hotel, Exmoor White Horse Inn in Exford
PUBLIC TOILETS In Exford village
PLAY AREA On Exford village green
ORDNANCE SURVEY MAPS Explorer OL9 (Exmoor)

The White Horse by Exford Bridge

the right. The path runs away from the river through marshy ground (follow yellow-topped posts), then turns right towards a gate and stile. Pass through the gate and turn right on the track to another gate at Lyncombe.

B Follow the track in front of the house house (right), and follow the bridlepath straight on towards Nethercote. Go through the next gate into open ground;

in the late 19th century when its church of origin, St Audries in the Quantocks, was rebuilt. Go through the gate/stile at the top of the hill (another path joins from the left). Keep ahead on the path which runs downhill across the field, signed 'Lyncombe'. The path drops towards the wooded valley of the Exe, over a stile/gate, then left along the field edge. Pass through a gate over a stream; keep straight on, keeping left of a line of gorse bushes. Continue downhill to cross a gate/stile in the wire fence next to the river, by Beach Pool. Cross two stiles and pass a ford on

the path undulates along the side of Lyncombe Hill, with lovely views over the valley to Road Hill. Pass through two more gates. *Just before the third gate note the path right which leads down to a ford and split log bridge over the Exe. This would shorten the route, but is only recommended for the intrepid.* Continue along the track through the third gate. At the next gate on the right turn right, following bridlepath signs downhill through the field, bearing half left towards the river. At the bottom turn left *(this part can be wet)* to walk through fields below West Nethercote, then through a gate to join the track. Turn right to cross concrete Nethercote Bridge.

C Turn immediately right through a small wooden gate, and follow the permitted riverside path. After 100 yds (91m) the path splits; keep straight on along the river's edge. The path curves away left to rise through bracken to meet a path at a T-junction; turn right and aim for the gate at the end of the grassy area. Pass through the gate, over two streams, and along the bottom of a sweeping field to pass through a gate to reach the ford.

D Turn left and follow the bridlepath as it turns uphill away from the river to climb steeply up Room Hill, with fantastic views over the Exe valley. At the top of the hill bear left, keeping about

Beech trees on Road Hill

50 yds (45m) away from the hedgebank on the left; when level with the metal gate turn half right **E** across the hill, following a line of hawthorn trees. The path here is indistinct, but curves left then right around the contours of the hill to pass a bridlepath sign for Exford and to lead onto Road Hill. Pass through a gate at the top of a line of beech trees, then through another. Keep straight on, with the hedge left, before dropping sharply to a junction of paths. The Iron Age hill fort of Road Castle lies between here and the Exe.

F Turn left on the bridlepath through the gate. The village of Exford, nestling between the hills, should be coming into view on the right. The settlement is thought to date from the Bronze Age, but little is known of its history until the

Exford Bridge is situated at a centuries-old crossing point of the River Exe. It marks the route of an ancient trackway that linked Cornwall with the Midlands, named the Harepath, meaning army road, by the Saxons. Although there is no evidence for its use for military purposes, it became an important trade route, and was a drovers' road in the 18th century. The economy of the village in the past was based on sheep farming.

Middle Ages. At the end of the field go through a gate, then downhill on a narrow path to cross a stream and through a gate at the end of Court Copse. Follow the alternative walker's route up the next field; at the top of the hill pass through the gate and follow the fenced path right. Pass through another gate and keep on downhill to meet the lane at Court Farm through a gate. Turn right to reach the middle of the hamlet; turn right, signed Exford and Winsford. Bear left immediately to cross the bridge over the Exe. Turn left and retrace your steps to the car park. ●

GPS WAYPOINTS

🖊 SS 854 383	**D**	SS 869 362
A SS 857 380	**E**	SS 861 360
B SS 868 375	**F**	SS 859 372
C SS 876 361		

How many horse's heads can you count at Court Farm stables?

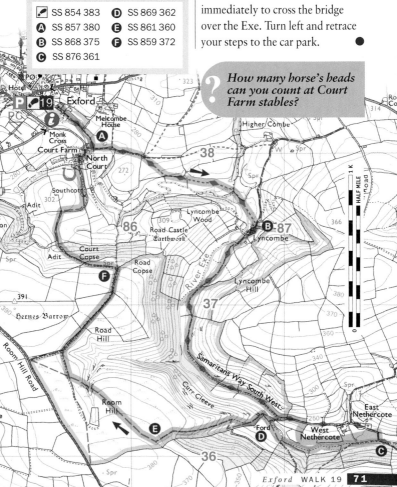

20 *Selworthy*

A glorious walk that offers a taste of everything that makes this area special: superb coastal scenery, far-reaching views from Selworthy Beacon, rushing streams and tranquil woodland paths… and a chance for refreshment in a perfect country cottage garden on the green in the National Trust's picturesque hamlet of Selworthy. Walking, rather than using your car, will at least mean that you deserve tea!

START West of Minehead
DISTANCE 5½ miles (8.8km)
TIME 3 hours
PARKING Second unmarked parking area on right of Hill Road, west of Moor Wood, on North Hill (signed from near Minehead Hospital, off Blenheim Road)
ROUTE FEATURES Steep climb towards Hill Road up Selworthy Combe

The peace, solitude and beautiful views from North Hill are welcome relief after the busy streets of Minehead. North Hill is signed opposite Minehead Hospital, from where you drive up Martlet Road, then St Michael's Road, through the twisting lanes of Higher Town. Note that the parking area is not marked on the ground.

Walk away from the road past a bench to meet the coast path, signed left for Selworthy.

Ⓐ Turn left and follow the coast path as it runs along the edge of North Hill. On a clear day the south Wales coast is clearly visible from here. Ignore an 'alternative rugged coast path' to the right; our

The **Holnicote Estate**, given to the National Trust by Sir Richard Acland in 1944, covers 20 square miles (5,180 hectares). A good place to survey it is from the car park opposite the church at Selworthy. This working estate comprises 14 farms and over 170 cottages, as well as Exmoor's highest point, Dunkery Beacon (1,703ft/ 519m) and the ancient oak woodlands in the Horner Valley. The fertile Vale of Porlock, with its lush patchwork of green fields and hedges, lies at its heart.

PUBLIC TRANSPORT None available
REFRESHMENTS Periwinkle Tearooms in Selworthy
PUBLIC TOILETS In Selworthy
ORDNANCE SURVEY MAPS Explorer OL9 (Exmoor)

Peaceful Selworthy Combe

more gentle route keeps a little inland and passes through a wooden gate to enter the Holnicote Estate, with fields right. Cross a concrete way and go through another gate. Follow the track where it runs a little inland to a T-junction after 1½ miles (2.4km) **B**. The coast path is signed right towards Hurlstone Point; there are views ahead of Dunkery Beacon *(see Walk 6)* and the wooded Horner Valley *(Walk 13)* to the left. Turn sharp left and walk to the trig point at the top of Selworthy Beacon 1,011ft (308m); enjoy superb views over the rolling Exmoor landscape. This area, including the cliffs, has been designated an SSSI. Walk downhill on a stony track away from the coast towards the road.

C Cross the road to enter the path at the top of Selworthy Wood, passing a low wooden barrier. Turn right to have a look at the little sandstone memorial hut, erected by John Barton Arundel Acland in memory of his father, the 10th Baronet, Sir Thomas Dyke Acland, in September 1878. On one of its outer walls can be found a really lovely quote, worth repeating here: 'In remembrance of the father who for more than 50 years took walks up this combe with his children and grandchildren, training them in the love of nature and Christian poetry, this wind and weather hut was built'. Sir Thomas had a habit of walking here on Sunday mornings and quoting poetry to his companions. Return to the bridlepath and follow it downhill past a sign to the Iron Age earthwork of Bury Castle (right), and then a spring. This pretty path drops downhill through light mixed woodland to cross a small stone bridge and spring, and joins a woodland track at a T-junction in Selworthy Combe. Selworthy Woods were planted by Sir Thomas from 1809, a block of trees being

> **?** *One Holnicote is here, in Somerset. Where in the world is there another Holnicote?*

planted for each of his nine children. Today the woods are threaded with a number of foot- and bridlepaths.

D Turn right downhill; the path levels off and meets a lane at a gate **E**, with Selworthy parish Church of All Saints above left. This remarkably light and spacious early 15th-century church is unusual in that it is still regularly limewashed to protect it from the weather. Most of the churches in the area used to be treated in this way. The church has an impressive 18th-century west gallery. Turn right for Selworthy village, NT shop

GPS WAYPOINTS

📍 SS 947 476   **D** SS 919 471
A SS 948 477   **E** SS 919 468
B SS 915 480   **F** SS 926 476
C SS 915 477

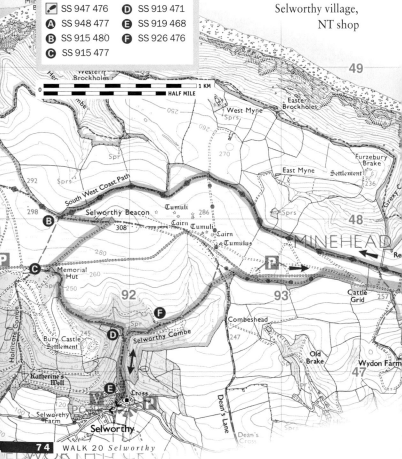

and refreshments. Selworthy is an idyllic spot – perhaps a little too 'perfect' for some – and very popular with visitors who come to look at Sir Thomas's work: in 1828 he had three medieval

farmhouses around the green restored to provide homes for his estate pensioners. The cluster of limewashed thatched cottages, with flower-filled gardens, rambling roses and hollyhocks, is quite delightful. Selworthy also boasts an impressive 14th-century tithe barn in the grounds of the old rectory.

Retrace your steps to **E**, then follow the bridlepath uphill to the spring and bridge **D**. Keep straight on uphill (signed Selworthy Combe). About 100 yds (91m) farther on fork left by a boulder along a small grassy path under silver birch and oak. At the edge of the woods **F** turn right and follow the path uphill through heathland, climbing steeply to reach a crossroads of paths. Walk straight over, signed 'North Hill'. The path runs east along the ridge past the back of a disused quarry (parking) to join the road. Turn right along the road; at the cattle-grid cross over and walk right through the gate. Keep parallel to the road, through the next gate by the cattle-grid (leaving NT Selworthy Beacon land), then take the track parallel to the road that runs through the viewpoint car park. Keep straight on for your car. ●

Further Information

Walking Safety

Always take with you both warm and waterproof clothing and sufficient food and drink. Wear suitable footwear, such as strong walking boots or shoes that give a good grip over stony ground, on slippery slopes and in muddy conditions. Try to obtain a local weather forecast and bear it in mind before you start. Do not be afraid to abandon your proposed route and return to your starting point in the event of a sudden and unexpected deterioration in the weather.

Some of the walks in this book cover moorland where adverse weather conditions can occur quite rapidly throughout the year. *Walks 2, 6, 10, 11, 14 and 19 should not be attempted in inclement weather.*

Otherwise the most difficult hazard likely to be encountered is mud, especially when walking along woodland and field paths, farm tracks and bridleways – the latter in particular can often get churned up by cyclists and horses. In summer, an additional difficulty may be narrow and overgrown paths, particularly along the edges of cultivated fields. Neither should constitute a major problem provided that the appropriate footwear is worn.

Global Positioning System (GPS)

What is GPS?

Global Positioning System, or GPS for short, is a fully-functional navigation system that uses a network of satellites to calculate positions, which are then transmitted to hand-held receivers. By measuring the time it takes a signal to reach the receiver, the distance from the satellite can be estimated. Repeat this with several satellites and the receiver can then triangulate its position, in effect telling the receiver exactly where you are, in any weather, day or night, anywhere on Earth.

GPS information, in the form of grid reference data, is increasingly being used in Jarrold guidebooks, and many readers find the positional accuracy GPS affords a reassurance, although its greatest benefit comes when you are walking in remote, open countryside or through forests.

Looking down towards Dunkery Beacon from Goosemoor Common

GPS has become a vital global utility, indispensable for modern navigation on land, sea and air around the world, as well as an important tool for map-making and land surveying.

Follow the Country Code

- Be safe – plan ahead and follow any signs
- Leave gates and property as you find them
- Protect plants and animals, and take your litter home
- Keep dogs under close control
- Consider other people

(Natural England)

Useful Organisations

Campaign to Protect Rural England
128 Southwark Street,
London SE1 0SW
Tel. 0207 981 2800
www.cpre.org.uk

English Heritage
PO Box 569, Swindon SN2 2YP
Tel. 0870 333 1181
www.english-heritage.org.uk

South West Regional Office
Tel. 0117 975 0700

Exmoor National Park Authority
Exmoor House, Dulverton,

Somerset TA22 9HL
Tel. 01398 323665
www.exmoor-nationalpark.gov.uk

National Trust
Membership and general enquiries:
PO Box 39, Warrington, WA5 7WD
Tel. 0870 458 4000
www.nationaltrust.org.uk

Wessex Regional Office
Tel. 01985 843600

Natural England
Northminster House,
Peterborough PE1 1UA
Tel. 0845 600 3078
www.naturalengland.org.uk

An Exmoor pony

Ordnance Survey
Romsey Road, Maybush,
Southampton SO16 4GU.
Tel. 08456 05 05 05 (Lo-call)
www.ordnancesurvey.co.uk

Ramblers' Association
2nd Floor, Camelford House,
87-90 Albert Embankment,
London SE1 7TW
Tel. 020 7339 8500
www.ramblers.org.uk

Youth Hostels Association
Trevelyan House, Dimple Road,
Matlock, Derbyshire
DE4 3YH
Tel. 01629 592600
www.yha.org.uk

Local Tourist Information Centres
Call 0870 40022300 to connect to
any TIC in the UK

Barnstaple: 01271 375000
Braunton: 01271 816400
Combe Martin: 01271 883319
Ilfracombe: 01271 863001
Lynton & Lynmouth: 01598 752225
Minehead: 01643 702624
Porlock: 01643 863150
South Molton: 01769 574122
Tiverton: 01884 255827
Watchet: 01984 632101
Woolacombe: 01271 870553

Lewis's Tearooms in Dulverton

National Park Visitor Centres
Combe Martin: 01271 883319
County Gate: 01598 741321
Dulverton: 01398 323841
Dunster: 01643 821835
Lynmouth: 01598 752509

Public transport
For all public transport enquiries:
Traveline: 0870 608 2608

Ordnance Survey Maps
Explorer OL9 (Exmoor)

Answers to Questions
Walk 1: You can get the key from
The Haven, opposite the lower
churchyard entrance (notice at
church)

Walk 2: You are on part of the
Tarka Trail. The paw print belongs

to an otter, commemorating the hero of North Devon author Henry Williamson's classic tale *Tarka the Otter*

Walk 3: Brown trout (information found on the board in the car park)

Walk 4: He was born on 7 June 1825, and died 20 January 1900

Walk 5: 698ft (313m) – answer to be found on an information board at the site

Walk 6: September 1935; the date can be found on a plaque on the cairn

Walk 7: Horses

Walk 8: 10 tons, and you will be prosecuted! Information found on the old Lynton & Lynmouth Lift Company sign on the bridge

Walk 9: An acorn

Walk 10: By AD1200 (answer on the car park information board)

Walk 11: There are young horses around; this land belongs to Waterhouse Farm (stud)

Walk 12: Miss B.K. Abbot and Auberon Herbert (information on a cairn by the path through the wood in point **C**)

Walk 13: You would have to fetch the key from Horner Tea Gardens (notice on gate)

Walk 14: You will be fined £5 (old notice near the war memorial)

Walk 15: Lady Harriet Acland: Lady Harriet's Drive, which runs from Pixton Park to Upton, is signed away from the dam at point **C**

Walk 16: Put up your tent!

Walk 17: C. Bulkeley in 1955 (found on the stone seat passed during point **B**)

Walk 18: They are painted pink!

Walk 19: At least two (stone ones on gate posts) plus however many are looking over their stable doors when you pass by (during point **F**)!

Walk 20: In New Zealand; John Acland lived there (as quoted on one side of the memorial hut passed at the start of point **B**)